Tales of an
AMERICAN ENTREPRENEUR
Journey of a Small-Business Owner

Michael A. Randazzo

AuthorHouse™
1663 Liberty Drive
Bloomington, IN 47403
www.authorhouse.com
Phone: 1-800-839-8640

© 2014 Michael A. Randazzo. All rights reserved.

No part of this book may be reproduced, stored in a retrieval system, or transmitted by any means without the written permission of the author.

Published by AuthorHouse 9/18/2014

ISBN: 978-1-4969-3654-7 (sc)
ISBN: 978-1-4969-3655-4 (hc)
ISBN: 978-1-4969-3653-0 (e)

Library of Congress Control Number: 2014915488

Any people depicted in stock imagery provided by Thinkstock are models, and such images are being used for illustrative purposes only.
Certain stock imagery © Thinkstock.

This book is printed on acid-free paper.

Because of the dynamic nature of the Internet, any web addresses or links contained in this book may have changed since publication and may no longer be valid. The views expressed in this work are solely those of the author and do not necessarily reflect the views of the publisher, and the publisher hereby disclaims any responsibility for them.

CONTENTS

Preface - ix
Introduction - xiii

Chapter 1   Taking Advantage of Opportunity in a Down
            Real Estate Market - - - - - - - - - - - - - - - 1
Chapter 2   Manifesting a Dream into Reality: The Start of
            Harmony Salon - - - - - - - - - - - - - - - - - 12
Chapter 3   Learning the Ropes - - - - - - - - - - - - - - 16
Chapter 4   Losing Employees for the First Time - - - - - - 18
Chapter 5   Advertising in the Beginning - - - - - - - - - 20
Chapter 6   Learning to Trade Stocks - - - - - - - - - - - 22
Chapter 7   Growing My Business - - - - - - - - - - - - - -26
Chapter 8   Our New Home - - - - - - - - - - - - - - - - - 38
Chapter 9   Opening a Second Location - - - - - - - - - - -41
Chapter 10 The Charlotte Job Summit - - - - - - - - - - - 46
Chapter 11 Selling Your Home in the Worst Market - - - - -49
Chapter 12 The Government and Small Business - - - - - - -51
Chapter 13 How You Make and Measure Profit - - - - - - - -53
Chapter 14 Financials: Charts of Accounts - - - - - - - - 59
Chapter 15 Saving, Investing, and Managing Your Money - - 65
Chapter 16 Losing Top Employees - - - - - - - - - - - - - 75

Chapter 17 Let's Take a Look at Customer Service - - - - - - -81
Chapter 18 Reading My Own Book - - - - - - - - - - - -87
Chapter 19 Over the Years Time Teaches If You Are Smart
            Enough to Learn- - - - - - - - - - - - - - - - - -92
Chapter 20 Being a Blessing to Those in Need - - - - - - - - -96
Chapter 21 What Next? -97

I AM WRITING THIS in the hope that you may learn from my experience as a successful small-business owner. I will tell you many of my best business practices. I will cover advertising, marketing, financials, leasing retail space, hiring and training quality employees, what to do when you lose key employees, how to borrow money, how to manage money, and many other key areas of business as they relate directly to the small-business entrepreneur.

Two things that drive me are the thrill of growth and the fear of failure.

PREFACE

I will go in depth and teach you key points to negotiate a win-win lease, showing you how important it is to your business that you cover every line in a lease, how to use some things as negotiating tools, and how to eliminate portions of the lease that can potentially cripple growth.

Many of you will connect with me as business owners who have struggled or are currently struggling with extreme stress. I am writing about my company, from starting it with no employees and a small location to now having been recognized for five years as one of the top two hundred fastest-growing businesses in North America in my industry. I started my business by myself with little money, and it has grown to well over a million-dollar business.

This book is written to help small-business entrepreneurs who are getting started and to coach those who have been in business for years. I will tell you from real-world practice what you are in for if you decide to go into business and show you what it takes to be successful.

Many of you may be looking at opening a franchise, and I want you to understand the level of commitment you will need to make in order to have sustainable profitability. It usually is not as easy as you may think, and the franchisor may not always tell you how much you will have to work at it.

I am writing this book to help anyone who wants to grow professionally and personally. I will be writing about personal investments as well, including purchasing a home, stocks, mutual funds, money markets, and retirement accounts such as a simple IRA.

Let me start by stating that I will not be telling my story with lots of fluffy adjectives. I will not be writing lines like this: "The day my top employee left was a cold overcast day. When I arrived at the salon, everyone was quiet. You could sense that something was wrong."

Oh, blah, blah, blah. Give me a break! That kind of stuff belongs in a fiction book! I don't like useless jibber jabber; I want just the facts. I am the type of businessperson that cuts to the chase. I want to be efficient and effective; I don't want to waste your time. That is the way in which I will be telling you my tales.

I will be giving you information I hope you can use, not a fiction story with lots of feel-good story-setting nonsense. I will be writing more along the lines of the following: "This is what happened, and here is how I handled it." The tales I will be telling are more like lessons rather than stories. I suppose I could have named the book *Lessons from a Small-Business Owner*, but I like *Tales of an American Entrepreneur* better.

I have owned my own business for over sixteen years. I use the word *business* because my business is profitable and provides me an income, with benefits like a retirement plan, paid holidays, and a paid vacation (although I don't usually take one). I have eighteen full-time employees, and I do not always need to be there working day to day as I would in a nine-to-five corporate job. Sure, sometimes I am putting in sixty to seventy-five hours a week for months, but most of the last six years, I have not had to work in the store day in, day out. I spend more time working from my home office than in the store.

I have invested successfully—and not so successfully—in stocks, mutual funds, and bonds, and I have been involved in multiple real estate deals. I have spoken publicly to large and small groups. I have been on the board of educational directors for two trade schools in my area. I have twice been nominated for the Global Salon Entrepreneur of the Year business award. My business is one of the top two hundred fastest growing in North America in the hair and beauty industry and has also been named one of the Charlotte, North Carolina, region's top fifty fastest-growing privately held companies.

As I write, I will be paralleling my business and personal life, telling my story as it was and is. I may move from one time period to another so you can see the results of investments, systems, and applications. I will write about challenges when they happened back when I first started my business and right now as I encounter them while writing this book.

I decided to write this book telling you the story of how I started my business. At the same time, I will be telling you about investments and opportunities as I encounter them. It is easier to write details of events, for example, trading stock or purchasing a home, if you write them as they occur, rather than trying to recall them only as events of the past.

I will give you lessons as I go, but you must also make connections and look at the entire story so you can apply my best practices in your life. You are reading about my life as a successful small-business owner, a husband, and a father. Stay with me, as I will be writing about what I did in the past—but at any point, this book may jump to present time so you will be able to read how I handle challenges in business and investment opportunities as they come up.

So, let's begin the story of the journey of this small-business owner.

INTRODUCTION

My name is Michael Randazzo. Currently as I write this, I own a salon/spa that has just been recognized as *one of the top fifty fastest-growing privately held companies in the Charlotte, North Carolina, region.* This award was printed in the December 4, 2009, edition of the *Charlotte Business Journal* and is also included in the *Book of Lists.* To be considered for this award, businesses must have been open for at least two years and have revenue of at least 1 million dollars for 2008. Out of the top fifty fastest-growing businesses, Harmony Salon placed number thirty-two.

About two weeks after this award, we received an e-mail confirming another award: we made the *top two hundred fastest-growing salons in all of North America!* This is the fourth time we have been honored with this award. This was published in the January 2010 edition of *Salon Today* magazine. For both awards, companies must submit documentation (tax returns) to prove the revenue claims.

I absolutely love my life. I feel blessed to have a great business that I enjoy going to and being involved in.

My wife, Lisa, and I have been married seventeen years, and we have two children. I place God at the center of my life, as he has always been in my heart and I have had a relationship with him since I was a small child. My favorite book I have ever read and continue to read is the Bible. I keep my marriage sacred and live as she and I, and then the world.

My family comes first. I do not think of what I want first but what they want. Work before play, and yes, I manage to do it all and have fun and play hard. To sum it up, I place God first in my life, and then family, work, and finally the world.

We live in a middle-class neighborhood. Our home is about three thousand square feet, with a three-car garage. In the backyard, there is a roof over the twenty-six-foot-long stamped concrete patio, with three ceiling fans, outdoor speakers, a separate area for my grills, a long counter (bar) for entertaining, and a walkway from patio to driveway. This is my man cave.

Our yard is wooded and nicely landscaped with lots of flowering trees and Japanese maples. The grass is green and thick. The yard is about two thirds of an acre.

I am not bragging about my home or things I have, but I feel you need to know my lifestyle to appreciate my journey. I believe that your lifestyle can help you achieve financial freedom or prevent you from ever getting ahead. I have a small mortgage on my house about equal to a car payment. I have no other debt, personal or business.

At this point, we are considering taking advantage of a down real estate market and buying what would be our dream home. I have looked at about a dozen houses and have made a bid on one. The house was foreclosed and is owned by the bank. I am offering below average for the per-square-foot sales price in the neighborhood and below the bank's asking price. I have run numbers every way, and I will have no problem making payments on two homes; I still do not have mine on the market. The key concern is the unknown. I cannot guarantee my income will continue to support these payments. Yes, I do not have a crystal ball, and like every other person, I cannot foretell the future. This is why zero debt is the goal. I will cover more of this later.

The world economy crashed in late 2008, and the stock market dropped so fast, far, and hard that everyone was panicked—even the so-called experts; some of them were actually crying on television. Many businesses are gone. The housing market has produced the largest number of foreclosures on record, and home values have plummeted.

This year my company has reached the highest profit since I opened over sixteen years ago.

No, I am not a billionaire or even remotely close, but the only debt I have is a relatively small mortgage. No, I do not consider myself financially rich; I do not make millions or even close to a million dollars a year. Everyone has his or her own ideas of what *rich* is and I suppose zero debt can be considered rich, but I believe that the overwhelming consensus is that being rich means having critical mass. This means that you have enough money so no one can determine what you do with your time.

I have applied financial discipline to keep us debt-free. We do not spend all our money. We drive mid-priced cars that we buy new and keep until they have high miles and are about to need major repairs. The last car I drove was a Volvo, which I finally replaced when it had about 315,000 miles on it. The car still ran well but needed some AC work and radiator repair. The company Lisa worked for gave a larger allowance for having a new car, so it made sense to get her a new one and I took her car. That is how we have done it for the past seventeen years. She now drives a Honda Odyssey Minivan and I do enjoy driving it with the family, but I won't be taking it when it is time to replace it. This one will be traded in!

My story is of someone who worked hard to get ahead. I have given blood, sweat, tears, and throw-up. During my journey I have spent many nights not sleeping and have been so stressed I have thrown up. Sometimes I had what I now call *success fear*, but originally it was just plain fear! I now recognize fear and find that fear is a key component of my success. Fear of failure keeps me going; it is a major driving factor that I connect with pride and turn into a driving force.

My life was not an easy ride. I was not born from wealthy parents or grandparents. We lived in what many people consider the lower-middle class on Long Island, New York. My father owned a small barbershop and had usually one or two part-time employees. He came from Italy to live in America when he was fifteen years old. He had only a third-grade education and could not read or write. My mom graduated high school and then went to work as a secretary. My grandparents on her side owned a small deli, and together they lived in an apartment above it. They worked fourteen-hour days six days a week, and on Sundays five to seven hours. They took off Christmas Day. They taught me a lot about commitment!

Lesson 1: My grandparents taught me to always give immediate and complete attention to the customer.

Lesson 2: You have to be available when the customer wants you.

My wife comes from growing up poor on a West Virginia farm; she did not have much at all. For Christmas she would get things she really liked, like bananas or cereal. She mostly had hand-me-down clothes from cousins and did not grow up in front of the TV as they barely got reception on only three channels.

Lesson 3: Stretch a dollar, and only buy what you need when you need it.

CHAPTER 1

Taking Advantage of Opportunity in a Down Real Estate Market

I AM STARTING WITH this chapter because it is happening as I am writing. I will tell the start of my business in the next chapter since I started my business many years ago. Remember, I am writing about both things past and as they happen so you can see how I did things and how I handle them as they happen.

I will fully admit that to write in this manner is a challenge. How do I bounce back and forth in time and keep your attention? The name of the chapter will help guide you as to where I am during the book. This is a book of my tales of how this American entrepreneur began and is running his business. It is about my journey as a small-business owner, and as a small-business owner, I will be telling you about major purchases like a house, a new location for my business, and how I invest my money.

It is February 2010, and it is now one week after we placed the first offer on the house I spoke of a few paragraphs before. We were thinking of taking advantage of the down housing market and discussed making what I call a lifestyle investment. So we decided to look at houses. I define a *lifestyle investment* as an investment in how you live that will bring greater equity to your finances when you sell it while providing an upgrade in your lifestyle. Examples of lifestyle investments are buying a home, remodeling your home, or buying a larger home or one that is located on more desirable land, perhaps a home on the water. It could be buying a second home in the mountains or on the beach or even in another part of the country. A lifestyle investment is one that will grow in value over time, so unless you are getting a great deal, a yacht or plane does not count.

We all make lifestyle investments every day; the problem is we don't take the time to look at what our lifestyle is. Do you like where you are? Do you enjoy coming home each day? Do you want to upgrade your living conditions by remodeling your home to make the living quarters more suitable for you? Would you like a bigger home? Are you thankful for what you have?

To the best of your knowledge, will the money you spend upgrading or buying a new home give you what you want and bring greater profit when you sell it? Sure, some people get satisfaction from reading their bank statement, but you can't live in a piece of paper. Sometimes you not only need to look at the interest rate of return or the ROI (return on investment), but also the lifestyle return. In our case, with so many high-dollar homes coming on the market at 40 to 60 percent less than the tax value, we decided to make that lifestyle investment.

I think most people may start looking and then get serious after they find something they like. This was a mistake in my case, and it caused me to have to do a lot of work in a small amount of time. However, I learned a great deal that I will share with you.

The first lesson here is to know your finances before you go looking. What can you afford? Speak with your accountant if you are not absolutely sure. What loan amount will you qualify for? Go talk with a lender and get a prequalification letter. This costs no money and requires no commitment from you; it is simply having a conversation with a lender and speaking about things like debt ratio and income. Know all your income, meaning if you do not already know exactly how much you have, add it up. Add up how much you earn, and if married, add your spouse's income. Then add up all the money you have in savings or investments. This will give you real data that will let you know up to what amount you may purchase a home for. You not only need to know how much you can put down; you also need to consider what you have available to make repairs, and you will always need something new, either new furniture, blinds, window treatments, plantation shutters, and so many other things.

You also need to consider your debt ratio. The lower you keep your debt-to-income ratio, the quicker you can become debt-free. I want to point this out now because when you go to buy a mortgage, a high debt-to-income level may result in a higher mortgage rate, or they may deny your request. Debt-to-income refers to how much debt you carry, meaning things like car loans, school loans, and any outstanding loans you owe, and what percentage these loans are to your income. Being debt-free is something I will go into as well, but for now I will just say that having zero debt is a big help for building wealth.

Remember, you may have to come up with closing costs, moving money, and other expense funds. You can shift some expenses to the seller, like closing costs and repairs, unless you are buying a foreclosure. In this market where banks are swamped with foreclosures, you may even get them to absorb some of these costs. They will tell you the sale is as is. But if you don't have cash for closing, simply tell them to pay your closing costs. If they are not willing, you can always try to find another opportunity where the bank may be willing to pay closing costs for you. Most sellers are willing to pay the closing costs, so even if you are purchasing from a home owner, you can request they pick up your closing costs.

Closing costs consist of what is referred to as prepaid costs and fees. Prepaid costs are the interest accrued from the time you close the loan until the time of your first payment, your escrow fees (which are your property taxes), and insurance. Escrow is used as a way for you to pay taxes and insurance each month in your mortgage payment. This can make it easier for you from a cash-flow perspective. Fees are usually called origination fees or loan fees charged by the mortgage lender.

By the way, don't simply agree to these charges. Tell your mortgage broker you want a loan that does not have any closing costs. There are also costs for credit reports, termite inspections, closing attorney's fees, flood certificate fees, title search, and more; sometimes the broker will have a few questionable costs in there. I do not mean to offend my mortgage friends—they do not all do that—but I do want you to be aware.

If you have bought a few homes and are familiar with the buying process, keep reading as I want to help the inexperienced as well as the experienced.

Most first-time home buyers get confused by the fact that yes, they are buying a house, but they are borrowing in most cases to do so. So what you are doing is buying money to purchase a home. Do not confuse this. If you are paying cash for the house, that is one thing, but most of us need to buy a mortgage. You need to negotiate the price of the home and the particulars of the home, such as repairs or what is staying with the home, like appliances or play sets, with the owner, no matter whether the owner is an individual or a bank. You need to negotiate the mortgage with the mortgage broker.

Many people are aware of the term *interest*, but they get a little confused as to what length of time they want to take to repay the loan. There are many products out there, from interest-only loans to adjustable-rate mortgages to fixed-rate mortgages. Interest-only loans are where your payment only pays interest on the loan and you don't actually pay off the loan. Remember, do not confuse this: you are not paying off your house; you are paying a loan.

There is also what is referred to as an adjustable-rate mortgage, or ARM for short. I have seen them from two to ten years. This means that the interest rate can go up or down. There are also ten-, fifteen-, twenty-, twenty-five, thirty-, and thirty-five-year fixed-rate loans. Usually the shorter the loan, the lower the interest costs are. However, the shorter the loan, the higher or more your payment will be.

Think of it as you borrowed x amount of money: if you take x amount of years to pay it back at x interest rate, you will have a monthly payment of x. Look at a loan calculator with an amortization schedule; it will show you how interest and terms affect the payment. Do some homework because when it comes to closing a deal, it is one thing to shoot from the hip; but if you want to hit the bull's-eye, being prepared will almost always get you better results.

DOES PREPARATION INFLUENCE FATE?

I found a deal that does not come along often in a lifetime; in the current economic situation, it is not as hard to find them, as we are in what is considered by many to be the worst economic depression our country has ever had, but it will not be this way forever. Remember the old saying "When opportunity knocks, open the door." If we look at history to predict the future, this deal is more of a once-in-a-lifetime opportunity.

Let me tell you this story. Two and a half years ago, I opened what was to be a second location for Harmony Salon. This was my third salon overall. During the time I was doing the build-out, I took a different route home and drove past a neighborhood that was to me so outstanding that I turned in. The gates were open, so I drove through, looking at beautiful European-styled homes.

I was in awe and immediately thought of how great it would feel to live here. The entrance had wonderfully landscaped waterfalls flowing into a small pond. It was a gated community that was detailed in so many ways. As I was turning out of this neighborhood, I saw another beautiful neighborhood next to it equally impressive.

When I arrived home, I told my wife jokingly that I found where I wanted to open my new location and told her about the homes I saw. Well, I went online and began to research the neighborhoods I had just visited. I read the description of the homes selling in the neighborhood and came to a line "with many homes soaring to well over 3 million dollars." I began dreaming of owning one of these homes and then came back to my then-reality. I told her we would have to forget that idea; I would need to open several more locations to be able to buy there. By now you already probably have guessed that the home we are bidding on is in one of these neighborhoods.

Let's look at the situation: the worst recession in our lifetime and arguably the worst in the history of the country. Stocks and housing had the biggest correction ever. The government has raised the debt to unimaginable levels, with numbers we cannot even begin to understand. We have a president that is trying to ram a socialist agenda down the throats of Americans without even letting them see it, instead of concentrating on reducing debt and helping the job market. We are being told that Iran may have weapons of mass destruction and will not hesitate to use them.

I think you can tremble in fear and would be justified doing so—or like a true entrepreneur, you could take control of the situation and look for opportunity.

This year my company has been the most profitable ever, in part due to the market collapse forcing me to look at every expense and drive my bottom line. If you look for ways to improve, you inevitably will find them; doing so helps create a better position for you to look for more opportunity, and this creates a cycle that will continue to help you grow so long as you continue to use financial discipline and take the initiative to capitalize on good opportunities.

Lesson 4: Always look for opportunity. Don't view down markets as a negative situation; instead, give thanks to God and look for what you can do to improve. Instead of fearing this crashing market, I immediately sought what I could do to improve my profitability.

I believe the housing market will return with a very slow and rocky recovery that will take several years, and I also believe that it is near bottom as we have seen activity in home purchases having gains in the past few months. Looking at the local real estate market in the Charlotte area and particularly in the price range I am looking at, I have studied several neighborhoods, and houses are selling and quick! A friend of mine just bought a beautiful custom home in a gated community, and in a few months' time, five homes in that neighborhood have sold. Looking at other neighborhoods of similar home value, I have seen a lot of activity. Contractors have begun to buy up unfinished foreclosures, taking them to completion and getting them market-ready to sell. Once they are listed, they move quickly. A house across the street from the one I am looking at went on the market, and in two days had a contract on it.

Down segments of the economy affect our business and personal investments in many ways, and you must learn to see the opportunity as well as the hardship. For example, this saying will never change: "Buy low, sell high." So why is it most of you will panic when the stock market drops? Instead, you should be looking for stocks that make sense to buy. The same applies to housing. Most people buy a house when the housing market is peaking, meaning you pay top dollar. When the market is headed down, it is the prepared that get to take advantage. Are you prepared?

Let's get back to this opportunity in the housing market. This was a million-dollar home according to the tax value. It was new and appeared to only need appliances and a few minor details finished. The list price was for just over $600,000.00. The tax value was about a million dollars.

When you decide you are going to buy a home, do not just go looking; go prepared to buy! Make sure you know how much house you can afford. Know what area you want to purchase in. when you go looking at houses and see one you like you must act quick in order to get your best deal. Do not wait for someone else to make an offer. If you use a realtor choose the most experienced realtor you can find. Interview several and ask them what price range of homes they have sold or purchased. What resources can they provide? Do they know good contractors? How about plumbers? Do they know a good HVAC company? Do they have good painters they can recommend? What kind of purchase are you looking for? If you think you will be buying an existing home from a homeowner you should have them do all necessary repairs before you close or if you are sure of what the repairs cost deduct this from the price of the home before you close. If you are buying or building a new home from a builder you most likely will not need repairs but you will need to negotiate your best deal and get agreement for any add on structure or cosmetics before you close. If you are looking to buy a foreclosure this is where a great realtor with resources can be helpful.

Being a savvy investor you must get the best deal you can especially when buying a house! Buying a home is large investment and for most people the largest investment they will make. You should negotiate all areas of the purchase price of the house. What is included with the house such as repairs, play sets, appliances, lights, Molding… get these items down as low as you can. For the most part have them include these things with no extra cost. You must also get the lowest price for the mortgage. Everything needs to be agreed upon in writing and completed before you close. I will say this again in case it did not sink in the first time "before you close" I will speak more on these topics but you get the picture think lower, less than, not as much!

When it comes to investments that large I think it best not to use friends that are realtors or mortgage brokers unless you clearly communicate with them all of your expectations and let them know you will need to get the best deal you can and they may have to lower their commissions or fees if necessary to get the deal done. Friends may misinterpret your intentions or you may not understand their intentions. Trying to get your best deal usually means you will need to be strong, confident, direct, and most of the time when you are with friends you are on a relaxed level so they may not react well to the business "you" and you might not appreciate their business side.

Experienced realtors can be very valuable if they have done many deals like the one you are involved in. When interviewing realtors, find out how many homes they have purchased or sold in the price point you are looking at. Find out how much experience they have with what you are looking for. Are you looking to buy a foreclosed property? How about a short sale?

Do not go just to look. If you find a house you like that is being sold at a discount, make an offer immediately! If you have not purchased many homes, a good attorney or realtor can help you draft your offer. By doing this, you can possibly avoid what happened to us.

We went back to look carefully at the house. I went in the attic and under the crawl space. Lisa and I took a flashlight and looked for any water at windows and ceilings. This should be done the first time you look at the home. Don't waste time. If you look at the home and like it, then get serious and look at everything in the house.

One of, if not the biggest, factor in whether and how much equity you will have in your home five or even ten years later is how much you pay for it. You must run comps on the property to determine its value. Comps are comparable recent sales. Comparable in square footage is the basic idea. Look at the sales in terms of per-square-foot sold price to determine the average price per square foot. Then look at the properties where some were foreclosed. Were they all completely finished, or did some need more work? What is the condition of the property you are looking at in relation to the properties on your comps?

When you get all this information, you can then get a better value for the property and make a more educated offer. If you have a realtor who is looking out for you, he or she can help you with the valuation if you are not sure how to do this. Once you place an offer, if yours is the first offer the seller gets, the seller may counter, giving you a superior position to any other offers that may come. In my case, I was the last of three. The bank countered the higher of the other two offers, so I had to rely on the information I had and not a solid counteroffer.

With regard to the condition, take a hard look; but remember when you place the offer, you can insert a dollar amount in the offer that you would be willing to accept if you need to do repairs. If the property needs more than the agreed amount, you can ask the seller to pay for the additional repairs or you can walk away. Again, a good attorney can draft an offer to purchase that will help give you the upper hand right from the start even if you are not well-versed in contracts. If your real estate agent has successful experience, he or she can also help.

I am not in the business of real estate, but I will tell you to be as thorough as you can. You never know; you may come up against a Donald Trump who will cream you if you make the slightest error. Trust me, there are a lot of people in the real estate business who are very skilled at it, so if you are looking to make a good deal buying a home, learn as much as you can. Just like buying a stock, the number-one rule is to buy low and sell high; never overpay.

My challenge was now doing all the legwork while trying to come up with a number that would take it, while at the same time not paying much more than the other offers. I also had to spend time in my business. I was interviewing candidates for several positions, training new hires, and all the other things I normally do at work, and it was tax season so I was also meeting with my bookkeeper and accountant.

I look at how better prepared I would have been had I done what I told you from the beginning. I made this great deal on a million-dollar investment, but it did take a lot of my time. The price I came up with was correct, and the bank accepted our offer. I had a home inspector out to look at the entire property immediately.

I also had HVAC, plumber, stucco inspector, electrician, cleaning crew, and irrigation out to check and give me estimates. Remember, I run a business and I look to save money everywhere. It is nothing for me to have multiples of people out one after the other or even at the same time to give estimates.

There were several times when I had multiple people from all areas at the same time. I work better when multitasking and think it also gets you a better price as they can see that you are on top of things and they will need to compete for your business. It is just as easy to call four references as two. I had to contact utility companies to turn on power, gas, electric, and water. When I turned the water on, I found that the tank-less water heater was broken and needed to be replaced. I also found only one return for HVAC on the main floor; this would limit the efficiency and cut the life of the unit.

Remember, I didn't own the property at this point but had the utilities turned on so I could properly assess the house. You could have tens of thousands of dollars in repairs needed that could make it a bad deal for you or even get you into trouble. Let's say you went ahead and purchased the home as is from the bank, and then found that you needed major plumbing repairs and later found even more problems. This could really cut into your profit.

I had multiple estimates within a day, giving me a better position for my counteroffer to the bank for repairs and also giving me a true out-of-pocket cost analysis and the ability to complete the work in a timely manner, scheduling work when I wanted it done. Some of the work could be spaced out so I would not have to take out money from savings, but instead could take from cash flow.

Remember that I am telling my story as it happened and going over the things that I did that I feel will help you to achieve what you want in life. I will also be inserting some of the challenges that I encounter while I am writing this book so that you can read firsthand how I handle the day-to-day hardships that occur in business. While I am writing this book, I will be telling you about investment opportunities as they present themselves so you can learn from my experiences in the past and as they happen, so stay with me as we move from past to present.

Remember these three letters: OPE—other people's experience. Using other people's experience is a great way to learn.

I am a strong believer in mentors. Look at people you believe are successful. They may be friends, family, coworkers, or even people you have seen speaking at seminars, or authors. In short, look at successful people and do what they did well and avoid what they did not do well. Look at unsuccessful people and don't do what they do.

I hope many of you will find these teachings extremely helpful, and if so some of you might be e-mailing me to coach you. (I could do a second book.)

CHAPTER 2
Manifesting a Dream into Reality: The Start of Harmony Salon

I WILL START FROM the beginning of opening my first location for Harmony Salon, which is also the beginning of what is now my marriage of seventeen years, which is still the best thing I have ever done.

We moved to Charlotte, North Carolina, in the spring of 1993. My wife, Lisa, was working in retail, and I was going to open a salon as I had been doing hair for the past twelve years and was now ready.

Lisa managed to get a job transfer two weeks later. She heard one of the managers was leaving and went to her district manager and told her she needed to be given the position. Lisa is the most driven person I have ever met. If you need something done, she has it completed immediately! Her district manager was glad she promoted Lisa, as under her management, her store reached the highest sales volume since it opened—and has never seen it since she left after she was recruited by another company.

During this time, I was looking for a location to open my business. We all know the number one, two, and three rule for real estate: location, location, location. This applies to residential, commercial, and business location. But the unwritten rule is money, money, money. You only get what you can afford, and I only had several thousand dollars. Looking back, I had a lot of other attributes I needed: determination, decent credit, youth, and drive. I was good at sales and at my profession. I was a hair stylist and particularly good at cutting; I had a good ability to give people new looks. I could find beauty in most anyone. I was good at doing styles for people that would really make them look great. I was also good at teaching others how to do it. I have always felt a great source of accomplishment from teaching others and watching them grow professionally. But still, I only had a few thousand dollars in my pocket.

I met a commercial real estate agent whose first words to me were about God. She asked me if I had a church that I was a member of and made some suggestions of churches in the area that I should try. I felt that we met not by chance but by purpose. She helped me find what I needed, a location that was easy to get to at the corner of two main roads. I knew that my business would come from referrals; since I could not afford a busy center with a lot of walk-in traffic, I wanted people to be able to find my salon easily. We found a location that was in a "dark" shopping center; this means that there were a lot of vacant storefronts, but it was a nicely kept retail center that was on the intersection of two main roads and easy to get to.

The store had been occupied as a salon, and the previous owner was in default of rent for quite some time. I was told that he did not pay rent and then just disappeared, leaving just about all the furniture and fixtures. The location had just about everything I needed: salon chairs, styling stations, a small front desk, mirrors, sinks, even towels. Basically all I had to do was order inventory and get a phone and outside signage. Well, I convinced the landlord that they should rent to me at a discounted rate.

I told you I was good at selling, and I sold myself to the landlord. I told them how I had been in the industry for many years and had been trained in hairstyling by some of the best in the world. I explained how I had taken classes at Jingles International, which at the time was located in the Empire State Building. Then I shared my employment history with them.

I explained that I had worked for my father for four years, learning a lot about cutting men's hair and how to run a business. My father had his salon for many decades. After gaining a good basic skill set doing hair, I left my father's business and went to a salon that did more color and more women. After one year I took a position at a very busy large salon doing haircuts on men, women, and children. Although I did not do hair color, the salon had several colorists that I worked with and watched and learned from. After a few years I was approached by the owner of the salon and asked if I would help teach haircutting to new hires.

I worked at that salon for seven years and really enjoyed being there. My boss was a great guy. He read the Bible, and many times would tell me the stories that he was reading and we would speak about how they related to our time or just how impressive they were. His name was Vincent, and we got along well. I always looked up to him as a good salon owner and person of faith. Many times there would be a group of us in the break room having church. We would speak about Jesus and read the Bible. This was very different from the typical salon environment. I remember going to several hair shows in Manhattan with Vincent and several other people that we worked with. I learned so much over the years when I was in the beauty industry working in salons, going to shows, and taking classes, that I felt it was now time for me to start my own company.

I also had a good credit score and provided the landlord with a business plan showing the rates for services and how I would market and advertise my business. We worked out a deal in the lease that the first three months were rent-free, and then I would receive a discounted monthly rent that would increase each year. The lease was a five-year lease, and instead of having the same monthly payment each year, it was reduced for nine months of the first year and then just added into the remaining four years. Doing the lease this way allowed me to grow some revenue and not have the pressure of high rent in the beginning. I also spread it out over four years so I would not see a large increase in rent but rather each year a small increase.

Lesson 5: You must have a clear business plan of how you will do business and how you will gain revenue.

You can learn how to write a business plan with books, DVDs, and videos. The best plan comes where you have experience in the business you are trying to start. You must be able to sell your business idea but also support it with numbers. You will need to have your price structure for your goods and services to show how you will generate revenue. Your plan should have an advertising and marketing budget as well, detailing what ads will look like and a sample of your marketing model. List revenue first, and then list all expenses. If anything is left, that is profit. Remember, you must list *all* expenses or you will not have a true projection.

CHAPTER 3
Learning the Ropes

I REMEMBER READING THAT you should always think bigger and talk yourself up when you negotiate with people. Read the *Art of the Deal* by Donald Trump. Donald is a master at this and has now made his self so much bigger than he was when he wrote it.

Learn the language of the people you are dealing with. For example, if you are borrowing money, bankers will speak of LTV; this means loan to value, how much they will be lending to you compared to the value of the purchase.

When dealing with landlords, they will cover many things, and the better location, the larger the lease document. Some leases will also have a requirement that you pay a percentage rent. *Never ever* agree to pay a percentage rent! If they will not strike it from the lease, walk away! Percentage rent is paid usually when the business revenue hits a certain agreed-upon number. You will usually have to provide monthly revenue numbers to the landlord, and when the revenue meets or exceeds the percentage rent revenue, you have to pay additional rent to the landlord. The landlords will try to confuse you or trivialize this by saying once the revenue exceeds the agreed-upon number, you pay a percentage of the revenue to the landlord. It doesn't matter whether it is based on the total revenue or just the revenue that exceeds that number; do *not* agree to percentage rent! Do not be fooled into thinking that the revenue seems so high you would be okay with paying more rent if you get to that level. It will not be easy for you to get there, and your cost for doing business will most likely increase. For example, you may have higher payroll costs, along with higher inventory and higher utilities. Paying a percentage rent, in my opinion, inhibits growth. Just don't do it!

Sure, I will play the devil's advocate and ask, "Well, what if the landlord is offering a low rent for you to start, and then will take a percentage once you get rolling?" I think it better to hold him to the low rent with no percentage, or offer a small increase in rent after a few years. When I say small, I mean small! Do your math and look at the rent cost for the year, not the month. Remember the accepted formula is to stay less than 10 percent of revenue for rent. In my opinion, there is no reason to give the landlord a percentage of your revenue; this can kill your business's growth and reduce profit. I advise that you strike percentage rent from the lease or go find another location.

Remember, many areas in a lease and in a loan are negotiable. Learn the language and speak it with them. A good way to start is to sort of repeat what they say in a turnaround, so if a banker tells you the maximum loan-to-value would be 80 percent and you want more, you might reply with, "If I have a high credit score, can I get an 85 percent LTV?" The more you speak with them, the more you learn. If you are speaking with them on the phone, ask where they are located and make a little small talk; this will put you on common ground.

When you get good at negotiating, take charge of the conversation. For example, when you are applying for a mortgage or build-out loan and they start to go through their prequalifying list asking you questions, you might stop them short and give them the needed details first. So it might go like this: "Mr. Randazzo, what type of—" And interrupt with, "I am looking for a thirty-year fixed loan. My credit score is _____, the purchase price is x, and I will be looking for x from you. I have been shopping, so I want to save us both time. I wanted to give you a shot at the business, so you will need to place a good offer up front, cut the app fees, and give me your best pricing. I am looking for no points, no origination."

When you speak in this manner, you control the deal—and they are trying to work for you, instead of just work you! The same goes with landlords. You need to gain the upper ground. You never should be over-cocky or disrespectful, but you should be confident."

CHAPTER 4
Losing Employees for the First Time

The first few years were brutal, as I imagine most businesses are when you start up with no capital. I worked many hours each week for about five years, not only in my business, but also working late into the night doing bookwork and what small accounting I could. I was in business for less than a year and had three employees. My schedule was full, and two of the three were busy as well. I was selling a fair amount of hair-care products and was able to make a small profit; however, I probably would have made more money working for someone. I had hired a couple employees that I had to let go; one was just plain not able to do the job, and the other was taking clients' numbers and offering to do their hair at home. In short, this is stealing.

For those of you who own a salon, you already know; and for those who want to open a salon, this is a fact you will have to deal with. You will spend a lot of time and money teaching your staff and growing your client base, and for the staff to steal from you in that manner can put you out of business. I suggest that you have employees sign a noncompete contract up front.

This was really a fifteen-hour-a-day seven-day-a-week job. I was working all the time; even when I was home, I had to do bookwork and develop marketing and advertising strategies. Well, the business grew, and I hired a few more employees. One in particular at first had some attendance issues, but Heather has turned out to be the best employee I could ever wish for and is still with me today.

One day my highest- and lowest-producing employees both just walked out. They gave me no warning; they just packed their stuff and left. I thought that they liked their jobs and were happy. Well, I guess not. I am including this because for all you new start-up businesses, I want you to learn from this. I went home that evening and could not sleep all night.

The next morning I got sick while I was in the shower—yes, I mean bent over and vomiting! My stomach was in a knot, and I was experiencing fear and a sense of betrayal. I had just bought a house and was worried about the mortgage payments, even though my wife was working and made enough to get us by. I have a strong sense of responsibility and have always felt I must provide.

Well, I went to work early the next day thinking that my other employee was going to quit as well, so I packed her stuff up. She came in, saw her stuff packed, and told me she had no intention of quitting, that she liked working there. Her words lifted my worries off my shoulders, and at that moment, I felt that I would make it. Heather is still working with me sixteen years later and has been a huge factor in the success of Harmony Salon.

Many people might have given up at this point and closed. Honestly, over the years I had times like this when the stress was very overwhelming, but I just kept at it. I would try to learn to control my fear and use it to propel me further. Sure, there were times when I thought I would close the business and do something else, but instead, I learned how to overcome to a point fear and stress. I learned from other people who were in business or management and from books and every opportunity I had. Sometimes I used good old-fashioned determination not to fail! I also learned from reading the Bible that no matter what I experience in life, God would be there for me, and it was eternity that mattered most.

CHAPTER 5
Advertising in the Beginning

I WAS NUMBERS DRIVEN and always looking at growing my revenue and at my costs. I understood that revenue minus cost was related directly to my income. One of the key costs I became very intimate with was advertising. I wanted to get as many clients as I could when I spent money advertising.

I instinctively knew that referrals were my best way to get them, so instead of placing an ad in a newspaper or magazine, I did a lot of advertorials. These were advertisements that told more about what we offered and who we were than just giving a percentage off or listing services. Advertorials can be written to look like an article or story, and by doing so, you can give more information to the prospect than you could with a traditional advertisement. Looking back, this led to getting some PR and having magazines do articles at no cost to me.

A great cost-effective way to get new customers is from your current ones. People are generally willing to recommend a business if they have a good experience and like the service or product you provide. Ask your customers for their recommendation; you can recruit them by offering a discount or membership points for referring customers. Back then, I offered clients 50 percent off a haircut if they referred three people. I developed a card filing system so I could track referrals and also log client information like history and color formulas. Today computers do all this and much more. We use an industry-specific software that is absolutely essential to running my business.

Lesson 6: Figure out the best way to get the most customers for the lowest cost. Always look at your ROI (return on investment). Track how your customers find you.

Today there are many software programs that will do this for you as long as you enter the information. I suggest doing so the minute a prospect makes contact with you. Once you compile enough data, you can then consolidate your efforts, reducing your expenses and increasing your market share.

Lesson 7: PR goes a long way, and you must maximize its potential Tell everyone all the time! Place your good news on your website and broadcast your message on your phone's hold "music." Make up in-house marketing material; tell all your family, neighbors, and everyone you meet. Send out press releases to newspapers and radio stations. Use Facebook or blog or tweet to get your story out there.

CHAPTER 6
Learning to Trade Stocks

THIS WAS THE TIME of the bull market, and stocks, particularly tech stocks, were soaring high. People began day trading in record numbers, and I was one of them. I read many financial magazines and newspapers to learn as much as I could.

I can remember one day having a long appointment cancel at the last minute, so I went home that morning and showed my wife the stock I had purchased the day before. I think it was Advanced Micro Devices, stock symbol AMD, and it rose that morning. Within about two hours, I placed my sell order and made more money than I would have made working at my store all week. I did this with companies like JDSU, Microsoft, Dell, and many others.

For a while, it started to go to my head. I made many trades that brought over a thousand dollars on each trade. I was trading stocks within a few minutes or hours, and holding some stock for a few weeks or a few months. I had to work many long hours in my business and still did not make that kind of money.

At one point, I considered just trading for a living. Well, after that short demented thought, I came to my senses. I think it was in part because I listened to Allen Greenspan speaking over the radio, and he warned of an unsustainable balloon in the stock market. I did some more research and found that the stock market might have been headed for a correction. So I decided I would concentrate on my business.

I did not reallocate as I should have. I should have looked at my portfolio and repositioned, going to a stronger cash side so that I could buy when stocks went lower. We did have a correction and stocks came down some, and then disaster struck!

We now call it 911. It was September 11, 2001, and we all know what happened. Terrorists flew planes into the World Trade Center and the Pentagon. I remember watching in horror as the first tower was struck by a large commercial jet. Then the second tower was struck. There were flames and smoke coming from both buildings and then I saw people jumping from the buildings. I kept thinking, why would a person do this to another person? This was pure evil. There is no other way for me to understand how people could do things like this to one another. The devil is running rampant and turning many people from God. This I know because scripture tells of these things.

I also know that Jesus was born and died for us. God gives us the final word, not the devil. Jesus defeated him by letting man make the final choice. Believe that Jesus is the son of God; accept him as your Lord and that is it: the devil is defeated. God gave people the power to live in unity and love. God gave us the choice to come to him freely in true love or to be demonic hateful creatures; it is our choice. The terrorists obviously lived in hate, misery, and rage, not trusting anyone but the demon they chose to accept. Jesus brought light to the world. He had compassion, love, and acceptance for all. How can love and acceptance be such a hard choice that people would doubt Jesus? It seems like a no-brainer to me.

The next few weeks were absolutely horrible for probably every person in our country, and I think even all over the world. Stocks could not trade, as Wall Street was under ruble. In the next few months, stock prices fell, and I can't say if I recovered all the money that I lost as it took a long time to rebound.

I do know that if I had paid more attention to buying solid dividend-paying stocks that would have been paying me dividends when share prices were down, that would have lowered the losses. Sure, I kept funding my retirement plan and the market did recover to post new record highs, but it only came down again with the housing crash of 2008-09.

In hindsight, when investing, I believe you should always keep enough cash on hand that will allow you to purchase when prices are down. In almost twenty years that I have been investing, I have studied market trends; and it is when the market is tanking and everyone is saying how bad stocks are doing that you have your best opportunity to make the most money. This can be done even if you do not have a lot of money—just allocate a higher percentage, like 20 to 30 percent, to be in cash.

One way for people to get started investing is by DCA (dollar cost averaging). By this I mean to buy stocks spread out over time, purchasing a stock every month. In theory, you could lower your cost, as you will be purchasing the stock at both upward and downward movements. DCA can be further enhanced by studying the price of the stock relative to the earnings per share. Tracking a stock this way will give you a more informed decision to make a purchase or wait till the next month. You need to be diligent in your research, and above all have patience if you want to make money.

DCA may be more effective if the investment is for more than ten years, such as your retirement.

You can also set up a purchasing plan through some companies to buy their stock through a dividend reinvestment plan known as a DRIP plan. When you do this, you can have the company debit your account monthly, and they will also reinvest the dividends paid in shares instead of money; this will grow your position in that company. You can also just buy the stock and just direct the dividends to be reinvested in more shares. By the way, if you are investing outside of a retirement account, the dividends may not be taxable until you sell the stock. If the stock is in a retirement account, such as a simple IRA or 401k, then dividends are not taxed until you begin to take withdrawals.

I think one of the first things you must learn to change is that you should be looking to buy stocks when the market is going down. Many people feel better when buying a stock that is on the rise, but once you learn about the company you are buying, you will feel better knowing you got it at a good price. If a stock is at its fifty-two-week high, you may want to wait for a pullback. Set a target price 5 to 10 percent lower than the high. I have had more success buying stocks that I knew more about than I did buying the ones that were going gangbusters and I bought them because I couldn't resist the temptation of how well they had been doing.

Lesson 8: Have patience!

Be disciplined and do not get greedy. Don't second-guess yourself if you sell a stock at a profit.

No one loses money when he or she sells at a profit.

"Bulls make money, bears make money, and pigs get slaughtered."

Be patient; you don't need to buy all at once. An alternative to chasing a stock that has already been overpriced is to look at the sector—let's say biotech. Instead of buying a lot of shares of one stock, how about buying smaller amounts of many? This way you increase your odds of getting the few that will take off and reduce the potential of having only one stock and it goes down. You don't always need a lot of shares to make money.

I also have seen that when the market tanks and you did not get out and are riding the wave to the bottom, you should just hold tight and ride that wave back up. If you are investing in solid companies, you should be okay. However, if the company is likely to show weakness or not be able to overcome the downside, then you probably should not have bought it in the first place or you should have done your homework and had stop losses in place to protect you.

I am not a licensed financial advisor but have been investing for a little over nineteen years, and I am sharing with you what has and has not worked for me.

CHAPTER 7

Growing My Business

My business was growing and I was learning; it was as if the stars were aligning for me. I look back at how I got to this point.

I met my wife while a friend and I were on a motorcycle trip. Back then my friend Bill and I lived on Long Island, New York. The ride was going to be from Long Island following the coast down to Myrtle Beach, South Carolina, and then we would head up to the mountains in Tennessee and ride on the Blue Ridge Parkway up through Virginia and back home to Long Island. We left Long Island and went to visit his cousin, also named Bill, in south Jersey. He was having a big party, and we arrived a little after twelve noon. There were a lot of people at the party as well as lots of food and beer. We stayed overnight and left the next day for South Carolina.

That day was absolutely great! We traveled the coast and took a ferry from South Jersey, Cape May, if I remember correctly, to Delaware and then rode on to Myrtle Beach, South Carolina. Around twelve midnight we pulled into Myrtle Beach and decided we would split up in order to find a nice hotel. Our motorcycles were equipped with CB radios so we could communicate and let each other know when we found a hotel. After only about five minutes, I found a great hotel right on the ocean and went in to see if they had a room. They did, and I quickly ran to my motorcycle to call Bill.

As I approached my bike, I heard him calling me. Bill told me he crashed and that an ambulance was coming for him. He told me he had some people there who had stopped to help him and told me where he was. So I went right over.

[Tales of an American Entrepreneur]

A young man and his wife were on their motorcycle and saw Bill crash. He was going to make a left turn, hit the unmarked median, and wiped out. Bill had plenty of road rash and was bleeding from several areas. He had some black and blue spots from hitting the ground as well, but otherwise he was okay. The emergency responders didn't think he broke anything but did want him to go to the hospital.

The couple that stopped to help went home to get their car so I could follow them to the hospital. After the hospital released him, Bill got in the car with Mike and Debbie, and I followed them back to their condo. We spent the night with them. Turns out they had two spare rooms.

The next morning I went out to get something from my bike, and I heard a girl say, "Hi, Mike." When I turned around, she said, "Oh, I'm sorry. You are not Mike." I told her I was *a* Mike, and we talked a little. I went back inside the condo, told Mike that I met a girl out front, and he said she lived right above them. Lisa was renting the condo for the summer with some friends and was from West Virginia. Lisa and I have been together ever since. Do you think it was fate that we met by accident?

We moved to North Carolina, and I met a great realtor who was able to find me a store that I could afford to rent. Now I was being approached by the right people, who were offering me an opportunity to move my salon to a location in a new shopping center that was being built across the street. This would be a better location with more traffic; it would include some big-box retailers, small boutiques, and a few restaurants. I would be able to build a larger salon that was more worthy in appearance of some of the PR we were getting. My business was getting great PR, and industry magazines were writing articles about our salon. We were also getting articles written in magazines like *Ladies Home Journal* and *Elle*.

For me this involved so much more than doing hair or even running a salon, as I now had to negotiate a deal in commercial real estate that involved leasing as well as building out the space. I also was allowed direct input in the design of the building with regard to the space I would occupy. I needed to make this deal affordable and knew that I needed to be able to make money when all was said and done.

I remember reading Donald Trump's book the *Art of the Deal* many years before, and in particular, one lesson that I always look to when making any purchase is that you get the best deal when you are willing to walk away from it.

Lesson 9: Do not get emotionally tied to the deal; look at it objectively.

You must focus on the deal. Will it do what you need it to do at a price that is better than you can get elsewhere? It is most important to run the numbers, add all expenses, and look at cash flow and how the payments will affect it. Will you place your family or employees in financial danger by spending all your capital and not having enough to weather the bumps that come along the way? This is called risk reward. How much risk are you taking? Do you have some evidence to support the risk, meaning is it pie in the sky? (Say, like writing a book?) Or does the math and knowledge you have suggest you will prevail? What is the reward? Will it justify the risk? Are you willing to take a loan on the equity in your home and possibly lose your home if you fail? If you have savings and don't use the equity, will it only cost you some money? These are questions you must answer yourself.

PICTURE YOUR DESIRE IN YOUR MIND

I believe that using visualization absolutely helps you get what you desire. Visualizing helps you set in motion your desires. When you are finally faced with the deal in front of you, you need to remove the emotion and look objectively at what you are about to commit to so you get your best deal. Dreaming about how you will look driving that new car or picturing yourself having breakfast in the new dining room or entertaining in the great room of the house you want to buy should be done *before* you get a deal in front of you. I believe this actually helps bring the deal. I believe that picturing what you want will help create it. I learned this from reading Arnold Schwarzenegger's book WINNING BODY BUILDING.

In his book he talks about closing your eyes and visualizing yourself looking big. See yourself as you want to look. Back then when I read his book, I was competing in martial arts and decided to put his theory to the test, so I visualized myself winning the competition I was going to compete in. On the day of the meet, I went in confident. I won each match in my mind before it even began. This was a big tournament with, as I recall, over sixty competitors. I was the first-place winner in my ring and placed third overall.

I decided that his theory worked, and to this day I have developed this practice and use it regularly. For example, Lisa and I would ride our bicycles through a neighborhood when we first moved to Charlotte, and we would wonder what people would do for work to be able to afford living there. I also used visualization to picture myself coming home to one of those houses and see myself pulling into the garage. I pictured pulling into the garage and getting out of a new Porsche or Mercedes. I found some high-dollar million-plus homes that were being built, pulled up the driveway, and tried to feel how it would be if it were mine.

Now I am looking at purchasing a new home in a higher-priced neighborhood. Keep in mind this did not happen overnight and this son of an Italian immigrant and his small farm wife worked hard for many years to get to this point. So it is important to get excited about what you want to acquire, but when you are approached with or entering the deal, you need to have solid numbers and guidelines. If you get too involved and too emotional before you know your limits, you can get caught up in the process and wind up overpaying.

When your offer has been accepted, then you can start to dream after you know your limits and after the main negotiating. Once the deal is signed, give yourself a pat on the back, have your family and friends over, pop open a great wine or bourbon, and celebrate. Do not look back and waste time second-guessing. If you did your job right, you now have cause for celebration. Enjoy the newly acquired possession!

In my situation, I had a good business going, with a measurable cash flow. By measurable, I mean constant and positive. I knew what I could afford in monthly rent payments and had worked out a formula of being able to pay rent with about 8 percent of revenue. During that time, 8 percent equated to about the amount the company took in on one Saturday. My concern was the amount of money for leasehold improvements. This was new construction; we started from dirt, so obviously there was a lot involved. Keep in mind that I was fully enjoying this entire process. I love negotiating and finding ways to make things happen.

RELOCATING MY BUSINESS

Well, here is the story of my first relocation of my business. This was the situation: a real estate agent came to me and told me he had an out parcel in the new shopping center that was being built across the street from where I was located. He needed tenants to get the financing to build on it. He was partners with a few others; one was a small construction company, or so he said.

I had never met him before so I had to trust what he was saying and do my homework to make sure he was legit. I knew I had some leverage—he came to me. I listened to what he was offering. He told me that Costco, Lowes, and other big retailers like Gap, World Market, and Circuit City were going to occupy space in the shopping center and that there would be some upscale restaurants and some women's boutiques.

I remember reading in the *Art of War* that if you face a superior enemy in strength and numbers, retreat and fight another day, so I responded by turning his language on him and saying I appreciated this offer but I was looking at another spot right now that was very attractive. He asked where it was, and I said that I was not going to discuss it but that I would tell him they were taking away the pain of moving for me and making it easy to get in.

What that meant was that they would be giving me a generous build-out allowance. A build-out allowance is when the landlord will actually pay for some or all of the cost required to set up the space you will be leasing. It is common for new shopping centers being built to only provide you with what is called a vanilla or eggshell. You get four walls framed, no floor, ceiling, electric, or HVAC—basically an empty space. I was interested in relocating, but I did not have much money saved and I do not like to take loans. My best plan of attack would be to negotiate a favorable deal and get the landlord to pay for all of the up-fitting costs. This would include the concrete for the floor, HVAC including ductwork, plumbing, phone cable, drywall, electrical wiring, and breaker box, and then have them pay for the build-out as well. I would get as much as I could for the flooring, lighting, water heaters, and building walls, including drywall and stonework.

I cut him short, thanked him, and told him I had to get back to work. I asked for his contact info, and we exchanged cards. I offered that we could get together and I would hear more of his offer. He asked to get together the next day, and I said time was tight for me—could we do it the week after next? I told him that he did have a good idea.

The next day I called a business friend and got some brilliant advice from him. He helped coach me on the lease side, and I will say that I learned a lot from him.

When you look for advice from a friend or someone you pay, like an attorney, make sure your advisor is great at what you need him or her to do. Ask for references. Ask if he or she has worked on this type of project before and at what scope and in what capacity. Quiz him or her a little. Ask for specifics, for example, what leases did you work on and where were the locations? What was the largest dollar-volume deal you made?

If you are looking for a business coach and the largest business he or she has worked with was one quarter the volume of what you are doing now, you may want to find someone who deals with companies larger than yours. Or if it is a lease, find someone who has worked with several at least the size in dollar volume as yours or more. Landlords in larger shopping centers with upscale national tenants will have more in their lease than a small off-the-path location, and a warehouse setting will be a little different as well.

A well-structured lease is, in my opinion, critical to the survival and growth of your business. It has a great effect on the profitability of your business. This is one reason that such a high percentage of businesses fail during start-up. Money spent on a seasoned business coach and an attorney who specializes in commercial leasing is money saved. Just beware not to throw money away. Before you ever open your business, you must think about everything in entrepreneurial business terms. You are no longer a technician or tradesperson, and you must think about profit before you even take in your first dollar.

By the time we met, I had worked up some numbers of what my costs might be to build out and up fit a new location. I made some calls to get figures on flooring, electrical, lighting, equipment, furniture, and retail displays.

When we met, I told him what I needed him to provide for the build-out and up-fit. He agreed, and we made the deal. During the construction, I was held up by the flooring and decided to go with a different product. I was going to do a wood floor, and the flooring guy kept telling me that the moisture level was too high in the concrete that had been poured five months before, not to mention we were experiencing a drought that had lasted several years.

A business friend told me to do an acid stain on the concrete; it was a lot less expensive, had low maintenance, and looked great. Edwin owned the Aveda distribution company and became my main vendor. Because of him (and the product), I eventually became an Aveda concept salon. Edwin was a great business partner, and I believe he truly wanted to help people grow their business and in turn he grew his.

I found a company to do the acid stain, and after a few returns to touch up, it came out beautiful and cost me thousands less. I overestimated the job costs, and they were being paid by the landlord. I cut costs midstream, and I wound up moving into a new location at a new and busier shopping center and placed thousands of dollars in my pocket to boot!

You may be thinking, "Yeah, sure he did. He got stuck on the rent." Well, this was not the case. I structured the lease with rent at a few dollars more per square foot than I was paying at the old location, but had three free months' rent. This brought my rent down for the first year to less than I paid in the old location.

My best advice is to do your homework and get actual costs; do not assume or ballpark. When negotiating, you will want to cover miscellaneous or unforeseen costs with a best guess, trying to allow on the higher side. If you are confident in the numbers, you can ask for more, but do not be so unrealistic that you don't get it.

I did know that even though I owned the business, what I really had was a job. I was doing hair five or six days per week and usually ten-plus hours a day. (This was the working in my business part.) I then put in many hours at home doing bookwork, payroll, marketing, and advertising. I knew that a job was not why I decided to open my own business.

About a year before the move, I started to shift my workload and outsourced my payroll; I found this to be a very cost-effective way to free up some of my time. Now payroll took me only about a quarter of the time I had been spending on it. Using the payroll service also helped accuracy. As you grow a company, you must have accurate financials.

I also knew I would need a bookkeeper. Ask your accountant and other business owners for referrals to find one. When you interview a bookkeeper, remember you are interviewing someone to fill a position in your company, even if you are just outsourcing and paying him or her to work a few hours a week.

Find out the obvious things, like how long he or she has been in business. Does he or she have a formal degree in accounting? But I think more important is what businesses does he or she currently serve? What type of businesses is he or she working with? How big are they? How much revenue are they doing? Find out as much as you can in relation to your business. You certainly do not want a bookkeeper who has only one or two clients that are all smaller than you or one that does not have a solid financial structure.

If you are a start-up, you will need to discuss how you will set up your chart of accounts. If you do not know anything about bookkeeping or accounting, regardless of whether or not you will be doing that work, you need to learn. You can learn about software like QuickBooks, and this will help get you started. If you do not clearly understand financials, as many business owners do not, then *learn*. If you can, do so before you open. If you are already in business, you must learn on the job, and there are many ways: take classes, speak with your accountant, hire a business consultant, read books. Reading this book will give you some information and ideas to help get you started in the right direction.

I can share information and teach you, but you must do the implementation. To put it another way, you can't have someone do your push-ups for you. You can go online; you can Google just about anything. Information is readily available today.

You can do this at night instead of wasting time watching mindless junk on TV. Peak performers use time wisely, and so must you. For example, it is a Saturday night, and we have company staying over for a few nights. Earlier we had friends over for dinner, and now everyone is sleeping. It is 11:00 p.m., and I am writing. I have also logged in to my computer at the salon to see how the day went and to get a forecast on next week's beginning numbers.

I will say this often: What are you doing with your time? I am not suggesting that you work 24-7, but I am suggesting that you should choose how to spend your day. If you decide that you just want to watch something on TV or some other nonproductive activity, do so, but be aware of how much time you spend doing so. When I outsourced the two components of payroll and bookkeeping, I had more time to work on growing my company—and when I needed it, I could enjoy some downtime.

After two years, we finally received national recognition. We were recognized as *one of the top two hundred fastest-growing salons in North America* by *Salon Today* magazine. This was a great accomplishment for my staff and me, one that I am very proud of. To be among the top two hundred out of so many salons in North America is really something. To think that I opened a business by myself, worked extremely hard, and now to be recognized in this manner is just great.

I need to tell you, especially if you are opening or own a small business, that at this point I have been in business for about eight years. This award did not happen overnight and did not come easy. I told you that I have been at times so stressed out that I actually got sick to my stomach. I spent many nights not being able to sleep and having such an overwhelming fear and stress it was beyond horrible. I worked so many hours week after week and month after month, I think most people could not begin to understand. If I calculated my hourly rate, I might have just as well been living in a third-world country.

Remember my grandparents? Remember how much and how hard they worked? Do you see a pattern? The people I know who have been successful in business, and by that definition have a profitable and long-term business, have all worked extremely hard to get there. Peak performers do tend to work a lot. To be successful in business is not easy.

By the way, it is twelve thirty in the morning as I am writing this book, and yes, I put in a full day at work and did not get home until 9:30

p.m. It was snowing, and on my way home, I passed a family walking on the road in the snow. I thought they must have gotten stuck as they were carrying packages. So I turned around and gave them a ride home. They were very nice and grateful, and I was glad to help. It was a great way to end the day. I saw several cars that were abandoned on the side of the road, some off the road in the ditch. Many people from the south don't have a lot of experience driving in the snow. We also don't have a lot of road equipment for snow removal. So it did take me a little longer than usual to get home.

IDEAS TO GROW YOUR BUSINESS

The better trained your employees are, the more valuable they are to your business. Think about it: an employee who provides a better service and knows how to sell the right products to customers is going to bring more revenue. In my business I tell my newly hired staff that when they are home, they should spend time putting money in their pockets by practicing new techniques or services instead of wasting time watching nonsense on television. The more you learn, the more you earn. When you have some spare time at home, work on improving your skill set. For example, you can practice foiling or cutting on your mannequin. You can go online to retail manufacturers' websites and learn more about the products you will be selling. I also suggest that instead of watching TV, stylists can watch how-to videos on YouTube.

Here are some things I did that really helped me grow my business. As Harmony Salon continued to grow, we again received the top two hundred fastest-growing salons in North America award the following year. After receiving the award, I knew I needed to create a website that would project the image of a business being recognized as an industry leader. At this time not every business had a website, but I knew this was the wave of the future, so I found a website designer online that was located in California and had them create www.HarmonySalon.com. I immediately began to promote it on everything I had. It went on business cards, T-shirts, advertisements, menus, and in-store marketing pieces—and we told everyone about it, every client, friend, and family member.

I worked on advertising to increase the client base, but instinctively knew that the heartbeat of the salon was not me being behind the chair doing hair. Sure, I could charge a good price for my services. I think at that time I was getting about fifty to sixty dollars for a cut, but by answering the phones and scheduling everyone that called, I was generating a lot more revenue. Think about how many people call your business and ask, "What are your hours? Where are you located? Do you sell such and such?" I made it my mission to get everyone who called to schedule an appointment. I would always engage the caller with questions about what he or she was looking for and be friendly, polite, and respectful. Oh yes, and always suggest coming in for services they wanted, but also let them know about other services we offered, be it facials, waxing, color, or haircuts. Many times they would add on to the services they originally called for.

I train all my front-end people to get every call on the book. If you are in any business that sells time, that is, if you schedule appointments, always schedule today before tomorrow and this morning before the afternoon. You have more time to sell tomorrow than today! When you get a call on a Tuesday and the caller asks if you have something for Friday, simply offer today. Do not make the mistake of thinking that people may think you're not good if they can get you today. There are many reasons why you may have an opening. You could have a last-minute cancellation or a no-show, or perhaps you just expanded your hours because you are so busy. Money in your pocket today is the game! It also allows you time to get money in your pocket tomorrow.

There are many things that I have done to get my business to grow. I will try to give you as many as I can.

A well-trained staff is paramount. When I say well-trained, I mean technical training, sales, and customer service. You should even teach them how to clean! You must cross-train employees in all these areas. Every employee that works for your company should understand all areas of the business.

In the salon business, we train the front-desk staff or people who are booking appointments the fundamentals of hair coloring. In order to schedule properly, they need to know certain things about the process. For example, you cannot just put color on previously colored hair to go lighter. First, the hair must be pre-lightened and then colored. Proper scheduling of appointments is effective in so many ways. The client is expecting to spend a certain amount of time with you and may not be able or willing to stay longer for a service that was not scheduled properly. Money is lost if the service just cannot be done due to incorrect scheduling.

Unhappy customers reduce revenue, so this just won't work. Even something so small as not showing every staff member, regardless of the position, how to fill paper dispensers in the restrooms can result in a customer who absolutely will not come back.

Every staff member must be trained in all business systems. Now obviously, specific positions will require more intense training in different areas, but you should get the picture. I recommend that you develop a new-hire training schedule and cross-train all employees in areas of customer service.

I believe no matter how much you do, you will not be able to please 100 percent of your customers. The key is to try to please as many as you can by eliminating the things that you can control; when you do that, look for those customer-experience issues you have not thought about.

CHAPTER 8

Our New Home

It is now the end of March 2010, and I have to tell you the outcome of the dream home that I told you of previously. We closed a few days ago at $45,000 less than my original offer. This was due to the appraisal coming back lower and I presented the bank with all the repairs that would need to be done. Work has begun to do the finishing and small repairs needed, and we will move in within a month.

I have listed my house for sale today, and although I will not get the money from it that I would have if this were a better economy, I would also not have been able to purchase our new property at about 57 percent of the tax value if it were not a poor economy. All things considered, even if we see an average increase in home value of 2 percent over the next ten years, which is less than the historical average, I have just made $115,000. In comparison, the home we were in at the start of this book would most likely return below the 2 percent, as it is a tract home at a competitive price point (meaning average) and I would most likely see only about twenty to thirty thousand dollars increase in the value in the same time period.

There are other things to consider also. Due to a new mortgage and substantially higher loan amount, I will be paying a lot more interest; however, I expect that I will see about the same amount going toward principal and thus continuing to build equity at the same rate. I will also see some much-needed tax relief that I was not getting from the other mortgage.

Yes, you can argue that a lifestyle investment such as this one goes against the principal of being debt-free, but I believe this: if your investment will make you more money and the debt is manageable this leverage can help increase your wealth. For me manageable debt would be to have your mortgage payment less than 25 percent of your gross income. This is assuming there are no other loans like car, or student loans. If you have debt other than a mortgage you should consider paying off those loans before taking on a higher mortgage.

I recommend looking at interest rates every month. If rates should drop and the cost of the refinance, meaning the amount the bank or lender charges for the loan, is not high, you could refinance and possibly save a lot of money and cut payments dramatically. All that is needed is for you to do the math to see if it makes sense to refinance. You would also do the math to see if it makes sense to pay the loan off early or invest the money you would have used to pay the loan off instead. For example, if you have a loan and are paying 3 percent interest, can you earn more than that by investing the money in a good stable dividend-paying stock? Remember, the interest may be tax-deductible, and that reduces the cost of the interest. If you pay 3 percent interest and then get to deduct the interest paid from your income tax, this lowers your cost of the interest.

Yes, I know that I cannot know where rates will be then, and this could negatively impact the refinance. But I am also implying that being able to substantially cut the principal should keep you ahead of rates. Most people think of mortgages in fifteen- to thirty-year terms, but if you take thirty years to pay off your house, you will pay up to two to four times the money (or the purchase price) depending on the rate. I also believe that you should have enough money in savings to pay all bills for six months if you are single with no dependents and one year if you are supporting a family.

Lesson 10: Protect against the worst-case scenario and grow the best case.

IF THE RETURN ON investment or lifestyle supports the manageable rise in debt, you can arguably and reasonably safely increase your wealth. This supports the old saying that it takes money to make money. What most people think this means is that you have to be rich to make money, but as I have outlined for you through this book, the term *rich* is relative, and I will say it again: regardless of your income, if you use debt to your advantage, it can help increase your wealth. If you misuse debt, you are playing with fire.

What are you doing with your money? Do you regularly burn it? By this I mean do you smoke? Do you squander it on frivolous junk? Do you even misuse your credit card to buy dust-collecting garbage, purchasing items that serve no purpose but you thought were cute or cool? This is a misuse of money and a habit of people who mostly do not get ahead. I am not saying never buy anything at all, but know and understand why and what you are making that purchase for. You should look at purchasing as debt. How much are you spending on nonessential things?

Well, it is now 3:30 a.m. on a Thursday night (Friday morning). We had a showing on our house the day after we placed it on the market. I have looked over the day's financials (by the way, at the salon we beat our month, which means we made our revenue goal for the month). I have read and answered e-mails from vendors, employment candidates, employees, friends, and business associates, as well as write this book. I have an 8:00 a.m. appointment, so I will now try to sleep for a few hours.

CHAPTER 9
Opening a Second Location

Let's get back to the salon. I have been in the new location for four years, and I am now looking at a potential new location, this time for a second shop. This is a new shopping center being built in a great high-density high-income area. By high density, I mean a lot of houses. I think at the time there were double the rooftops and double the household income of my current location. The center was to be a large destination center consisting of cotenants that would support my business, such as Banana Republic, Ann Taylor, White House Black Market, and Coldwater Creek. The plans were to also have small boutiques and several restaurants, ranging from McDonald's to high-end fine dining. In the middle of the layout was a grocery store that would bring daily and weekly traffic; the perimeter was to be some big-box retailers like Target, Marshall's/Home Goods, Off Broadway, and several others. There were a few banks and a gas station and many other retailers. This was exactly where I needed to be.

I began negotiating with the landlord at the point when several businesses had opened—Harris Teeter, Starbucks, and a few others. Target was to open shortly. I knew I did not want to be one of the first to open because there was too much construction and not enough business at that point; however, I did want to pick the best spot in the center.

The lease was very complex and consisted of many pages (probably as many as the new health-care bill that was rammed down our throats in a matter of a few days). I knew enough about leases to begin reading and highlighting areas of concern. I also brought on a local attorney, and through my retail vendor Aveda, I worked with an attorney from out of state. I cannot cover the entire lease, but I will speak on areas of major concern.

The landlord wanted me to be open seven days per week. I did not want to be committed to that number of hours, and I do believe that a business should be closed one day a week so that you can spend time with family and worship without interruption. God commanded us to remember the Sabbath and to keep it holy. This was a loving commandment from a loving God. He created the earth and its inhabitants in six days and rested on the seventh. God knows that in order for us to balance our lives, we need to rest for a day. He also knows that we will lose our way if we do not keep that day to strengthen our relationship with him.

Think about your life, and I bet sometimes you can be so busy and have so much going on that you cannot fit it all in. This is one reason that some marriages fail, some parents do not know their children, and some people stray from God. When you take a complete day to rest and be with family and worship, you strengthen solid core values and relationships that are, in my opinion, critical to having a purpose-filled, love-filled, and balanced life.

You may be wondering why this is the first topic I speak of about the lease and why I am not talking about how much the rent is. If you are, you still have a long way to go. I suggest you keep reading. Rent is a given, and you should try to get the lowest rent possible. Do I really need to say more? There are so many other negotiable variables that most people are not familiar with, and this is what I want you to learn.

The leasing agent, who was also the landlord, asked for percentage rent. The landlord wanted a percentage of my gross sales above and beyond rent. They will usually give you a line like this would only apply if the business grosses over a certain amount in revenue. No matter the case, *never* agree to a percentage rent; it is crippling to growth. Do not be a small thinker and say, "Well, if my business ever does that much, I will be happy to pay." You will most likely work harder than you imagine and endure more stress than ever, not to mention that as a small business you are already paying a very high tax rate.

I immediately struck this from the lease. There was no need for me to seek counsel. I simply took my pen and crossed through each line pertaining to percentage rent and then put an X over the paragraph. I do want to point out that when I spoke with the landlord, I told him with strong conviction in my voice that this was not negotiable and must be entirely struck.

One major cost when starting a business is the build-out. You typically find what is called a shell when going into a new construction center. The landlord provides you with four walls and a ceiling. You have to design and create your store. This is when you can spend way too much and ultimately wind up designing and building a store for someone else when you can't pay the piper. Understand that the landlord figures in rent against build-out costs, and you need to know what that is in order to pay the least rent and get the most money for the build-out. Yes, I said you get money for the build-out! Negotiate with the landlord what you need for the build-out.

You should contact a great architect who can help you determine costs or price things yourself. Get bids from several companies providing the work needed—HVAC companies, good electricians or lighting companies for lights, plumbers, concrete company, every business needed for the leasehold improvements, or your general contractor (GC) can provide itemized costs.

First you will need to get the dimensions of the footprint and find a designer or team that can work with you to design your store. This is very complex, and you need to think not only about the look, but also practical use and customer-experience flow. Every detail needs to be covered. What happens when a customer walks in? Which way do they walk? For some strange reason, when people walk in the door, they turn to the right. How and where will they be greeted? Where do you place your retail furniture and equipment? What colors do you want? What kind of lighting? Where will the restrooms be? Keep in mind that there are building codes that you will need to meet as well, ranging from how much energy or lighting you can use, to access of restrooms and handicapped access and many others.

A good architect, design team, or commercial GC will help with a lot of this, but you should *never* blindly go along and let them do everything. You have to control your costs and should be familiar with every aspect. If you want your business to be successful, you need to understand when and where you need to put the money. I use this analogy: if you are building a boat and you miss one seam, when you take it to sea, it will sink. If you build the boat too top-heavy, it will sink in rough water.

Know your finances and think about making money. You may not need the froufrou fine-art thingy to hang on the wall. How long will it take you to make that money back, and is that item really going to help your business or could you find something less costly? You also need to consider what kind of business you are. Do you want a low-priced or high-end type of business? You may need to spend a little extra if you are attracting high-end clients; however, if you are thrifty, you can buy things that look expensive but are not.

You are going into business with the intent to make money and support your family, not going on a mindless decorating and spending spree. Shop everything. Hunt for the best prices on your equipment, fixtures, furniture decorations, lighting, and such. For everything you purchase for your business, you must pay as little as possible. Think about it this way: if you structure your lease properly, you will have the landlord agree to pay a certain amount for the build-out. Get him or her to commit to a solid dollar figure. Do not allow verbiage that will allow him or her to pay less if the cost comes in less. Start making money before you even open.

I am not telling you to just try to stick it to the landlord! What I am saying is shop and try to find better pricing. You have the build-out money from the landlord, and you have a budget of approximately how much you will spend. Now hunt prices, cut spending, and shop everything! Oh, one more thing: don't purchase from any company that can't guarantee delivery by a specified time. You can't just purchase your equipment based only on price. If they do not deliver, it will cost you by delaying your opening. Going into business is that intense, and you must be frugal yet not too frugal.

You will need to either contract this yourself by subbing out all the work or hire a contractor. You will need electricians, HVAC, plumbing, drywall, and many other professional service businesses, like computer network companies. You can also hire a general contractor (GC), who will build you a turnkey store; he may also provide an architect.

If you hire a GC, you will need to work closely with the supervisor and stay on top of everything. If you are savvy, you can still get your own subcontractors to do some of the work even if you use a general contractor.

Request your general contractor to itemize his or her proposal. Immediately shop those items you feel confident in. For example, shop the HVAC, electrical, or flooring. You can then go back to the general contractor and say you will be hiring someone to do the floors or HVAC. Then you can have him or her draw up a contract stating the work he or she will do. I suggest that you place a clause in the agreement stating the date he or she will turn over to you a completed store or your opening date, and fine him or her for every day after that date you are not open.

If you do hire other companies to do some work, you will meet some resistance from the general contractor to this agreement. Be fair and give the sub-companies the same type of agreement, that they must complete their work properly and in a certain time frame. Be prepared for delays and things going wrong. Anticipate this, and it will be easier to handle when they come up. Be proactive and stay on top of things.

CHAPTER 10
The Charlotte Job Summit

It was now March and I had been invited to a job summit by the mayor of Charlotte, North Carolina. To be honest, I did not know what to expect. The invitation read something like he wanted to get small businesses together to discuss what role the government could play in helping put people back to work. President Barrack Obama wanted to use money that was being paid back from the banks to create another stimulus plan, this time designed to help small businesses. I phoned the mayor's office and told them I would be there, not knowing how it would go and thinking I would just be lectured to on what they wanted to do.

When I arrived to the conference center, I was surprised to see a continental breakfast provided for us, although it was we the taxpayers that were footing the bill for it. The summit began with the usual introductions, and then they had one of their economists speak to us. Being on the left side of the aisle, he proceeded to say that the creation of wealth, particularly the rise of home values, was what created the economic crash. Well, I looked around the room to see people's reactions to his speech and did not see anyone showing any sign of anything. No emotion, no reaction whatsoever. When he was done, he invited questions, and I stood up immediately.

I asked him to clarify his statement about wealth. I stated that it was not creation of wealth that caused the crash. I said that true wealth is measured by the amount of debt ratio carried by that wealth and to say creation of wealth leads to economic downfall is not correct. He agreed.

I then asked him to address the increase in home values and stated that the rise in home values in itself will not lead to a crash if the increase is due to supply and demand and created by true market value. He agreed.

I then stated that it was the 100 to 125 percent loan-to-value (LTV) and the criminal cheating involving builders, real estate agents, mortgage brokers, and some other well-heeled dishonest people buying and selling between themselves that led to the artificial increase in home values; however, even more important, it also led to an even faster rise in the debt ratio. This created people with no equity or even negative equity. Coupled with Fannie Mae and Freddie Mac and the government forcing banks to loan people money to buy homes—people who did not have the means to support those loans—this is what created the crash!

He responded with, "Well, you may have had more foresight than us." He agreed that the crash was due to many factors that were hard to identify at the time, but that the excessive rise in debt led to the extreme correction that we were now facing.

Then I asked him to clarify for me the fact we agreed on: that it was debt that created the crash, and then the government went and did the very same thing that got us there in the first place and increased debt to unheard-of levels! He responded by saying that we could handle the debt. I guess he missed the whole point.

Well, the summit broke out into smaller group sessions to exchange ideas on what would help us and, in particular, what would help us hire. I was in a room with a representative from US Airways, a few bankers, and some other small-business owners. We spent almost two hours speaking about the task at hand. I have to tell you that it was a great experience to see how one idea grew another and then how we developed each idea. I will say I was impressed and proud to be part of that session.

I suggested that one way to help us hire was to give us a substantial incentive tied to payroll, give the business a tax credit for each employee hired. Or cut the business portion of the payroll tax. I explained that it took me about three months for a new hire to be profitable and that if they wanted me to hire more people, I would need help. There were some other ideas, like reducing government, cutting government salaries, and making the Bush tax cuts permanent.

When I arrived home, I went online to see what was being said about the summit. One blogger wrote: "Just what we need: a bunch of businessmen who probably sent the jobs overseas in the first place telling the government what to do to help them more."

People just do not get it. Business does not send jobs anywhere. It is government that forces business out of the country by regulating and taxing them so they must leave to stay in business. For the record, I never sent jobs overseas nor have I ever had the ability to do so. The businesspeople I was with were local small businesses, and they do not send jobs overseas. Consider this fact: small businesses employ over 80 percent of the people in this country. So in regard to hiring, it will be small businesses that light the spark that will start the fire and fuel jobs growth to the point that you will begin to hear of big companies hiring many people.

By the way, now in 2011, the president wants to extend "his tax cut" to the middle class. Remember the payroll help we asked for? Well, the government lowered the employee portion of social security from 6.2 percent to 4.2 percent. How in the world does this help me get the money I need to hire more people? We all know social security is underfunded, and they are telling us it won't be there when we retire, so how is this a good thing? Could they not have done this a better way?

It is not that difficult to see that they really hurt us with that move. Their argument here is that people will have more money in their pockets to spend, which by the way supports the argument of lowering taxes for all income levels. Yes, I said *all* income levels. "Ooh, those evil rich people shouldn't have a lower income tax," you might say. Yes, they should. More money in their pockets will lead to purchases that have a greater economic impact. A flat-screen television will employ a few people to make it, but a yacht will employ many more, including the flat-screen television employees. A camera will not need as many employees to build as a car. Window blinds will not employ as many people as a summer home. Now are you starting to get the picture?

No matter how much a person makes, the government takes over 20 percent of honest hardworking people's earned income, calling it tax—when it's more along the lines of slavery or thievery.

CHAPTER 11
Selling Your Home in the Worst Market

I WANT TO TAKE you back to our house. We listed the house on a Wednesday afternoon. We had a showing Thursday and two on Friday, and had a contract on Saturday with the first people who looked at it. In short, we sold our house in eight hours in what is said to be the worst real estate market in our country's history. We sold it for four thousand dollars less than our asking price and only because that is what it appraised for. The point is that I did not carry two mortgages for a long time. This turned out to be a very clean deal. We purchased our new home, moved in, and closed on our old house within a month.

I want to point out that when you are thinking about trading up, a well-calculated plan will likely reduce risk and can increase the payoff. When you are thinking about selling your home, here are some things to consider. Get rid of your stuff. Put away, sell, or give away all the things lying around that you are not using. Make your closets bigger. Give away to a charity all the clothes you have not worn in a year; you will not wear them. Touch up the paint in your house. Even if the colors are not neutral, the house will look much better if the paint is fresh. Clean your house professionally inside and out if necessary. Does it need pressure washing? Pay attention to the curb appeal. Plant some flowers, pull the weeds, and edge.

Everyone thinks that their home will sell because it is special. Well, it is not in the eyes of an appraiser. In my case, I believe what sold my house so quickly was a large, well-landscaped private wooded lot with a high-end outdoor living area that no one in my price point or even a few hundred thousand dollars more had. I know this because as I was planning for the sale, I went online and searched all the houses in the price range within seven miles to see what they looked like.

To prove my point, my neighbors four houses down, with the same floor plan, took about five months to sell their house at over, I believe, fifteen thousand less. Now, looking at the appraised price, they both came close. Mine was slightly higher. I did have more money into my home, certainly more than the difference in the appraised value, so again, in this market they really only look at square footage. The extras are what make the sale come quicker.

CHAPTER 12
The Government and Small Business

Remember that I am writing this book in past and present context and do jump from time period to time period so you can see how investments work out as I am writing.

It is now June. We are settling in our new home, and I am concentrating on my business. I have hired several more employees, and most of them qualify for the new payroll tax incentive. Yes, that is right. If you recall, I told you about the job summit, and I am impressed that it was not just PR and photo ops.

There is a new form each new hire fills out. Basically if they have not worked in the past sixty days and are legal US citizens, your business gets a pass on the company portion of payroll tax less social security and F.I.C.A. In addition, there is an incentive of more than $1,100.00+ if you keep them employed for over a year. This is a little help for my company, and I am going to try to hire right to the line of profitability. In short, I will employ as many as I can in line with what my needs are. I think that the government should also get the word out so other employers are aware.

Wait a minute. This is what we were originally told about payroll help: that government wanted to help small businesses hire, but somehow now it transformed into only the employee paying 2 percent less in social security tax. This obviously does not help small businesses hire. President Obama is telling everyone that this reduction in social security tax equals about a thousand dollars for the average family. So let's look at this: employees are paying less into social security. This can't be good for their social security retirement. Business does not receive a break. Govco (the government) is now taxing that money as income, so they take from our retirement and use it to fund what? They also count on you blowing that money so they can recoup a little on the sales-tax side. This is not my idea of helping the public. Many small businesses that hired thinking they would be able to reduce the wage increase with a payroll incentive will not get that incentive, and this will impact their bottom line. This is why I stress always have some money saved for emergency situations.

Here are some other things the government did to try to "help." They decided to pass a health-care stimulus that businesses needed to look into, as they did not make it widely known. Small businesses could get back money the company paid toward health-care premiums for employees whose earnings were under forty thousand dollars per year. The rules were: the employee must work at least thirty hours per week, and the company must pay at least 50 percent of the premium. Employers with twenty-five or fewer employees may qualify, and premiums paid for dependents are not eligible. The credit is two hundred and fifty dollars per employee, not to exceed premiums paid. You will need to confirm this tax credit. I am not sure if it applied to all states or when they will end it, but as long as the employee fits these criteria—even if they are not currently employed, as long as they worked during the tax year—your business may be eligible for the health insurance tax credit.

These incentives can be viewed by the businessperson as a great tool for growth, or they can translate into more profit for the company to help secure the jobs created. One thing I will tell you is to check each year with your accountant, payroll service, insurance broker, and bookkeeper for any and all tax credits, as they change frequently. Remember to ask all of them, as one may not be aware since our tax code is so complex and changes so often.

CHAPTER 13

How You Make and Measure Profit

MANY BUSINESS OWNERS DO not fully understand how they make money, especially if they are working in their business in a revenue-producing position. They tend to get caught up working in their business, and many times this produces nothing more than a job, which they usually do not make a good profit at. A lot of businesses operate this way. The owners are operators trapped in a business where they must work many hours but ultimately do not earn or have the potential to earn what they wanted to or thought they would when they bought in. The other scenario is owners who purchase franchises in businesses that they know little to nothing about and find that after opening several stores, they are putting in a lot of effort with little or no return.

To start, let's examine why you are opening a business or are already in business. Did you open with the desire and thought of earning a lot of money? Or are you a skilled craftsman who went out on your own because you thought you could do it better? The first reason for getting into business may involve a type of franchisee who may not have done the proper homework and had false hopes of getting rich. The second reason we see many times with people who are good at what they are doing—maybe a pizza maker or a plumber, yes maybe even a hairdresser. They open a business and many times find themselves working ungodly hours and not making decent money. Even if they worked about fifteen to twenty hours a week less, the hourly pay would be close to or less than minimum wage.

My first rule is *Do not open a business that you do not know well.*

In order for start-ups to grow, as an owner you must know the inner workings of that business. Think about it: Why would someone who does not know step one about cooking open a restaurant? Now there are probably some shrewd businesspeople that run successful restaurants, but who are they? We all know Emeril Lagasse and Bobby Flay, famous chefs who also know how to run a business. If you have no clue how to do hair, why would you open a salon? I can tell you firsthand that this business is especially hard if you do not know how to cut and color. At least if you open a burger shop, customers do not go there for specific employees. Do you know the name of the person who hands you your Big Mac at the drive-through? I bet you know a lot about the person who does your hair. What I am saying here is that some business models make it easier to replace employees like the person at the counter at McDonalds. But if you own a restaurant and you are not a chef and your chef quits, this can cripple your business.

Even if you are a true master at whatever business you are in, you need to have a mix of master of the art and master of finance. You need to learn both, and as you grow, you will need to learn more of the business side. So why wait? Why not start right now? After you read my book, go out and purchase three more books relating to business. Take a look at your specific need and become a black belt in it.

I read a book many years ago that was simple but profound. It was called *Zap, The Lightning of Empowerment,* by William Byham and Jeff Cox. The reading was easy. It was in storybook form, but it was very useful, especially for all of you who want to do it all—who want to micromanage and delegate, but after you delegate, you do the work yourself instead of letting the employee handle it. When you have a business and want it to grow, you will find that you *cannot* do everything all the time. You need to hire employees to do specific jobs and should have a training process that duplicates how you want things to be done.

One great thing about using OPE (other people's experience) is that you get a sort of shortcut showing you potential pitfalls to be aware of and also some tried and tested things that work. So I encourage you to read and learn as much as you can and use a business coach.

So, we have established a few possibilities of why you are opening or have opened your business. Now let's look at the color green—how do you make money? Well, first you need to sell; you need to generate revenue. Revenue is how much money your business takes in. We need to generate revenue to get our business to start breathing; the more revenue, the bigger the breath. Once we are able to breathe, we also need to be concerned with our heartbeat. We need to get the blood pumping. Do not be solely concerned with revenue. Many business owners spin their wheels trying to reach revenue marks and fail to see the entire picture.

Revenue is not paycheck. Sure, it will play a big part in it, but it is *not* paycheck. Remember that you have to subtract all expenses from revenue and *if* there is any money left over, that is profit. Profit is the heartbeat, the blood of the company. But profit is still *not* paycheck, and you must read this carefully.

Profit is not paycheck. Paycheck is in-your-pocket spendable money! Profit is *not*. You must look at profit as a sort of guideline to paycheck because they do go hand in hand: if profit is high, so can your paycheck be. But if you take all the profit and do not leave enough behind, this can be a disaster!

When I speak with people about business, I tell them that when you own a business, you never quite get to enjoy all the fruits of your labor. What I mean by this is that even though your company will pay tax on profit, you cannot take and spend all of it. You must leave enough behind in the business to weather the storms that come out of nowhere.

Especially if you are in the start-up phase—and I categorize start-up as the first three years of business—you will have things come up that can cripple your business. We can have big increases in oil products, and if your business consumes these, it can cut deep into profit. Equipment, yes, even new equipment, can break, and you may still have a warranty on it, but how do you operate until it is repaired or replaced? What if you can't hire a much-needed employee or if one quits?

What if all these and more happen at the same time? *Do not* think that they won't; remember, chance favors the prepared. The more cash you can accumulate, the better prepared you will be. You may be able to purchase a competitor's equipment for pennies on the dollar due to poor planning on their part! This is something you should start to work on immediately. Not having enough capital has been the downfall of many businesses. Even if you have been in business for many years, do not forget the golden rule of reserve cash—have some!

Lesson 11: Profit is not paycheck! Be disciplined and keep some money in your business. I use a multiple of about four to five times payroll and rent combined, and some believe you should keep double that!

Now let's look at how you can increase profit. If you are in the first year of business, don't spend any money unless you have to! Sounds easy enough, but you would be surprised at what people spend their money on. You have read earlier in this book about doing your build-out and watching your start-up costs. Do you need to buy the gold chandelier with the diamond inlay? Okay, I am exaggerating, but to make a point, think about what you are putting into your business. Who knows? You may need that chandelier; you are the one making the decision.

Some expenses are a given, but what about things like advertising? Many business owners think they have to advertise. I am not saying never advertise; I am saying as I have before, think about who your customer will be or is. What are the most cost-effective ways to reach him or her? How about paying your customers to bring you more customers? Start a membership or rewards program. Do an old-fashioned card that you stamp each time they send you another customer, and after X amount of referrals, give them Y. You can partner with other businesses in your area, and maybe give their employees a discount.

Just think about it before you spend money placing an ad in some garbage magazine thinking that people will flood your store. Sure, if you do your homework and place the correct ad that is designed to get people in your door, you may see some ROI. Track all your advertising, and don't advertise again with ones that you did not make money on.

Now let's look at inventory. Your vendor, sometimes even the franchise, will want you to keep a boatload of inventory. This is how they make money. The more you buy, the more they make. There is an art to retailing for profit, and you must learn it. The two rules that I have front and center are (1) if you don't have it, you can't sell it; and (2) if it has not sold in a month, you don't need more than two, and if it has not turned in more than three months, you don't need it.

Next rule: *Do not overstock your winners.*

Many retailers get lost in the "Wow, this product is selling, so I need to keep lots and lots on hand." Why? Why keep more than you are turning between orders? Yes, I know you will not want to run out, but let's say you are selling twenty-four of a particular item in a week and you order every week—why keep fifty in stock? That means that you are not selling twenty-six each week. Sure, you do not want to run out of it, so you will want to stock a few more than the selling number, but think about it: if that item costs you ten dollars and you are not selling twenty-six per week, you are in essence losing $260.00 per week. That is $13,520 a year. I suggest, rather, that you keep no more than thirty in stock; if you have thirty and sell twenty-four, you have six left, so you order twenty-four. I don't recommend only keeping twenty-four on hand because you will have none on the shelf before the order gets delivered and processed and you could miss sales.

Now, how many items are on your SKU list? Even if you only have fifty different items you sell, if you overstock each item the same as in the previous paragraph, that is three thousand nine dollars a week you are losing! Yes, I know that you probably don't stock that many of every item so you may be losing less, but what about the business that has over two thousand items? Even if they are only over by ten items, they are out twenty thousand dollars a week.

To be successful at retailing, you must look at unit sales every week. You must count every item every week if possible; if not, I suggest to cycle count as often as you can—how about monthly? Cycle count means instead of counting all inventory each week, you rotate and count certain domains one week and then rotate and count others the next. Track the top-selling and the bottom-selling items. This will identify low- or non-selling items and also identify top-selling ones. No, not the top and bottom twelve, but the top 50 percent and bottom 50 percent. Products are either selling or not. Yes, you need to consider items that come in and out of cycle, such as seasonal or fad items, and this is why we count and look at retail reports. Reducing inventory without cutting too sharply will greatly help with cash flow and ultimately lead to more profit, and yes, you figured it out, a bigger paycheck.

Do you have employees on the clock? Look at how and when you need them; do not give them more hours than needed. How about sending them home early if they are not busy? You may think, "Well, it is only a half hour." Wrong! For example, the employee earns ten dollars an hour, he or she works full–time, and you have ten employees. Multiply five times ten then times five days a week then times fifty-two weeks, and now you are at thirteen thousand dollars.

Now I will point out for those who just don't get it, I am not saying you treat employees horribly and cut hours every chance; on the contrary, many people are thrilled to be able to leave early. What you must beware of are the ones who will purposely be standing around an hour before their shift ends, as well as the employee that constantly clocks out after his or her scheduled time.

CHAPTER 14
Financials: Charts of Accounts

When you set up a business, you will need to set a chart of accounts; in short, you need to break down all of the business expenses. This is done by charting out each check that your business writes and allocating it to a specific category or account. Let's look at an example: when your business purchases cleaning supplies, you might put that into janitorial. If you purchase pens and computer paper, you could allocate this to office supplies.

Yeah, okay, so maybe you already have your business set up and are recording expenses to charts already. Let's look at how to properly allocate so you can truly see each segment of your expenses.

How are you breaking up payroll? Are all the checks going under one account? Depending on your business, this could be sufficient, but I suggest that if you break out key positions, you can use the information better. For example, if you have managers, you may want to view them separately; or if you have sales professionals and hourly workers, you need to break them apart. This way, you can look at each department to see if they are producing or costing.

How about the scenario I have in the hair and beauty industry? We have two sources of revenue: one is service, and the other is retail. How do you measure your true profit from each? Let's talk specifically about retail; however, this also applies to service as well, but just for clarification, we will use retail. It should be obvious you must break out the product cost.

Here is an example:

Retail	$350,459.89
Retail cost	$157,706.95
Profit	$192,752.94

If you use this example, it shows that you have leftover or profit of $192,752.94 right? *Wrong!* To get a more accurate picture of your profit, you need to break out the direct cost of your retail. In my case, I pay a commission to my stylists for retail sales; this is a big expense and will change that number considerably. Now it looks like this:

Retail	$350,459.89
Retail cost of goods	$157,706.95
Retail commissions	$21,207.59
Profit	$171,545.35

Now you can go even further to get a better snapshot of your true cost. How much do you spend directly on shipping for your retail? If you find it appropriate, put that right underneath commissions. For those of us who want to know to the penny, you keep going till you have all the expenses listed.

Now back to the practical side. In my case, I do not see any value to shipping my retail and my professional products separately as this would incur added shipping charges, so I look at my retail cost and professional product cost and allocate the percentage.

So for an example, if I have $157,706.95 in retail cost and $100,248.00 in professional product cost and I have a $2,150.00 shipping cost, I can allocate the shipping cost between the two according to their percentage of the total. Dividing retail by the total shows it is a little over 61 percent; dividing professional product by the total shows it is almost 39 percent. So I allocate 61 percent (1,311.50) of the shipping cost toward retail and 39 percent (838.50) in shipping to professional product.

Once I have my cost broken out, I then have all of the other expenses listed. This includes everything else: rent, advertising, finance charges, accounting, utilities, and so on. At the end, you will either have profit, or if it is negative, then loss.

Do not get so caught up in where a certain expense belongs. Simply define what it is when setting up your charts. Many accounting softwares already have a generic chart set up, and you can customize it to fit your specific needs.

I speak with a lot of small-business owners who don't have a clear understanding of financials. Many of them just write checks for six months to a year and then hand them over to an accountant. If you do this, how can you know where your business stands financially? Is your business profiting? Or are you losing money? Sure, one way to tell is when you do not have any money in your business checking account; however, this equals failure!

ACCOUNTING SOFTWARE

Let's take QuickBooks. I am not a QuickBooks guru and this is not an in-depth lesson on how to use QuickBooks, but I do want to give you some basics and get you started in the right direction. Keep learning!

Your chart of accounts is a list of everyone your business writes checks to. Don't worry about future vendors; you can add more once you get going. Every time you write a check, the software will prompt you to set up who you are writing this check to; is it a vendor, employee, or other? You can then log the detailed contact information about the payee. You will only have to do this once as the software keeps a record of this information, and then when you write a check, as you type in the first few letters, you will see the name come up.

When you are writing the check, at the bottom it will ask you where you want to allocate this money to. In other words, what kind of expense is this? Advertising, janitorial, office supply, or perhaps the check is to you? In this case, if it is not your paycheck, then it may be considered a shareholder distribution or paying yourself back money you have loaned the company to get started. Check with your bookkeeper or accountant if you do not know the best way for you to take money out of your business.

QuickBooks keeps a chart of your accounts for you, and by doing this, it will take this information and generate your profit and loss statement. By properly recording your expenses, you will be able to see where you are spending money. This, believe it or not, is how you track cash flow.

Cash flow is, I believe, one of the least understood parts of the financial equation. Cash flow is the balance of spendable cash that your business generates. To measure cash flow, you will need some time to get all the information necessary to generate benchmarks to measure your monthly profit and its relation to your average balance in your business bank account. Using the information in these reports, you can track areas you may need to cut back on. You will be able to see if you are taking too much money out for yourself, or maybe you are spending more than you need in certain categories or not enough. For example, do you think that office supplies are too high? Or does it look like you are not spending enough in marketing?

Once you have a year under your belt, you will be able to compare this year and last and see how your expenses, as well as revenue, compare. This must be done month to month or week to week. By doing this, you can start benchmarking, which helps with forecasting or goal setting.

Let's look at cash flow a little more. Chances are that your cash flow will fluctuate weekly as your bills are paid. Remember, not all your bills come due and get paid at the same time, and you will no doubt have higher and lower amounts paid each week; this means that you will have to watch how much money you take. Make no mistake: you can also not take enough. The right balance is the key to maximizing your business's financial health. Take too much and you could put yourself out of business, but take too little and your money is not serving you.

What good does it do you to have too much money sitting in your business checking account or even a business money-market account? How could the money serve you better? Think about reinvesting in new equipment or a larger location. You could pay off bills or step up donations to charity or church.

The point is, once you can predictably and safely measure cash flow, you should have a purpose for the money. Remember, you will pay tax on your profit even if you do not take it as a distribution, and currently small business in America pays the highest tax rate in the world. Why would you make money on which you pay taxes and not have a purpose for it?

I know this may sound odd, but many small-business owners do not plan what to do with their money and wind up leaving it sitting in the business checking account, or worse, spending it foolishly and just wasting it. If this is the case, at least look at better options for investing. Can you earn more money in another relatively low-risk account like a money-market account or a certificate of deposit? This is where a good financial planner or perhaps your accountant could lend some advice.

To their own demise, many owners spend every penny and wind up either just getting by or going out of business. Ultimately you should do your homework and decide what you want to use the money for. Do you need more or better equipment? Do you need a larger space? How about another location or more employees? Then there is the personal side. Does it make sense to purchase a larger home, new car, or perhaps a second home? You may need to reevaluate your children's college savings plan or your life insurance. Have you laid the financial building blocks to secure your family's future? As you increase your earnings, you should reevaluate your company's and family's financial strength.

UNDERSTANDING FINANCIAL REPORTS
WHAT IS A BALANCE SHEET?

To make this easy, a balance sheet simply reconciles assets and liabilities.

Assets are bank account, receivables, inventory, and fixed assets such as equipment, machinery, furniture and fixtures, signage, software, and vehicles.

Liabilities are payables, loans, and credit card debt.

Your balance sheet gives you a snapshot of what your company's assets are.

THE PROFIT AND LOSS REPORT

Known as the P&L, this tells you where you stand from the revenue and expense viewpoint. It is an indispensable tool to view your company's health. With proper accounting, you can view your revenue and expenses. I look at my P&L reports and measure this year's month against last year's month, this year-to-date against last year-to-date, as well as this quarter against last year's quarter.

The profit and loss statement summarizes revenue and expenses during a specific amount of time. The P&L will show the company's ability to generate profit by increasing revenue and reducing expenses. The report starts with the company's revenue and then subtracts the costs of running your business. This includes costs of goods and services sold, tax expenses, operating expenses, and interest expenses. On the bottom of the report is net income, known also as the bottom line. This is the amount of income that your business has generated; however, remember as I have told you earlier, "profit is not paycheck," meaning you should not spend all of your profit.

You will need to decide what accounting method you will use. Will you use cash or accrual? Check with your accountant to decide what is best for your company. Using the cash method, you record revenue (or income) when you receive it from clients. You record expenses only when you write the check. This method is a little easier, but does not, in my opinion, give you the best picture. For example, if you ordered and received inventory in May and paid by credit card, then received the credit card statement in June and paid the credit card statement that month, you would have to record the expense for the inventory you ordered in May under June expenses. This does not allow you to see true monthly expenses, nor does it allow you to take the expense when it happened.

Using the accrual method, you record income when the sale occurs if you are rendering a service or at the delivery of a product regardless of when you get paid. You will record your expenses when you receive goods or services, even if you don't pay for them till later. Example: take the same scenario from the above paragraph. You order and receive inventory in May and pay in May by credit card. The statement comes in June and you pay it. You will be able to take the expense for the inventory in May. This allows you to look at your financial reports more accurately each month, and it also allows you to take expenses in the year that you actually had them instead of pushing the expense into the next year, thus reducing your taxable liability. In short, you pay less taxes because you properly recorded your expenses.

CHAPTER 15

Saving, Investing, and Managing Your Money

I FEEL IT IS necessary to include this chapter, as so many people I speak to always have questions regarding this subject. Sure, everyone wants to make more money, but so many people can't seem to get ahead even if their earnings go up. I will state first and foremost that you must have a purpose for the money you earn.

First comes saving. For all you who want to jump the gun, get hip, buy stocks, and get rich, I am here to tell you that is not generally how it works. Before you invest, you first need to take care of the following things with your money. Each pay period, designate your savings first. Start by taking a small percentage of your paycheck and put that in some type of savings account. Ask your accountant or financial advisor what is best for you. A good benchmark is between 10 and 20 percent goes to saving. This money is designated to build money to cover six months' worth of your total bills, including rent or mortgage, all utilities, loans, and insurance payments. If you have children, you may want to build eight to twelve months in savings.

Next, tithe; this is generally looked at as 10 percent. If you are a Christian, tithing can be found in the Bible, or ask your pastor. In the Old Testament, people were instructed to put away a tenth of their earnings and then go to another town and spend it—basically take a vacation. There are other references to cattle and giving every tenth one to be sacrificed to the Lord. People were commanded that as they counted, they were not to replace the one counted as the tenth with a lame or smaller cow; each one counted as the tenth was to be given. From these teachings we now give one tenth to God. So I suggest you pray and listen to where God wants you to put those resources. It may be church, charity, or even to help your parents or other family. Once you get your savings built to your level of six to twelve months' income, you would then switch this order and tithe first.

After you have tithing and savings, pay your bills. If you have anything left over, put it to savings; and when you have saved enough, start an investment account for retirement, like an IRA, 401k, or if you are self-employed, a simple IRA. So in short, 10 to 20 percent to savings, 10 percent to tithe, use the rest to pay bills, and any leftover put back to savings—do not blow it on stuff you don't need. Be smart not to include wasting money on junk or impulse purchases as bills; if you do, you only cheat yourself because this wasteful spending is what keeps so many people back.

Do not ever charge anything you can't pay in full when the statement comes at the end of the month. If this sounds hard, then maybe you should be considering whether you are being a good steward with your money. There is a way to use a credit card properly, and you need to know the difference between a charge card like American Express and a credit card like Visa/MasterCard. A charge card must be paid in full each month; you do not carry a balance forward into the next month. A credit card allows you to carry a balance and is therefore extending you credit, or in short, a loan, on which you pay a high interest rate. I want you to think of a credit card as going to the bank each month and borrowing money at usually a higher rate than you would pay for any other loan.

To properly use credit or a credit card, you must not carry a balance on that card for any purchase that is not absolutely necessary at that time. Pay the balance each month and do not charge if you can't pay. If you have situations that need to be addressed immediately—let's say you need to purchase or replace equipment for your business or have to replace the air conditioner in your home, this is the only time I would extend the credit for up to three months and only if you don't have extremely high interest rates on your credit card. By this, I mean pay the credit card off in three months. If your credit card interest rate is high compared to a business loan, then take a loan and you won't pay as much interest. Keep in mind that the loan terms should be appropriate for the amount of the loan. In other words, do not take a long-term loan for a small amount because you wind up paying more interest! If you need a water heater or another repair on your home, I would rather you take the money out of savings to pay than put it on credit and pay high interest. Just make sure to pay yourself back, putting money back to savings immediately.

After you get your savings goal accomplished, then let's talk about investing. What are you investing for? First designate a portion of your income for retirement. I suggest 8 to 10 percent. Yes, you can pull some from your savings as you have now reached your savings goal. Once you have six to twelve months' income in savings, if you don't have enough income, you can take the savings percent down a little to make up the percentage you need for your retirement account. The beauty of investing for retirement is that you can do it on a tax-deferred basis, meaning that for every dollar you contribute, you lower your taxable income by that amount up to the allowable limit that your retirement plan and income level allow. Check with your accountant or investment advisor for the amount you can contribute.

So now that you save that amount of money in taxes, you have money left from the tax savings to designate to a savings account for items like a new car, vacation, or whatever you decide to put it away for.

So many young people say, "I will never get enough saved for all that." I ask them this: "How would you eat an elephant?" The answer is one bite at a time. The key is to take the first bite. If you don't start, you will accomplish exactly what you said, and you will never get anything saved. In short, you accomplish nothing and never have anything worthwhile. The next thing you need to do is give it time. You will be surprised at how much you have saved after just one year. Once you start investing and earning dividends, you will really appreciate the power of compound investing. Remember, I used percentages in specifying the goal, so when your income goes up, so do your contributions.

When you get to the point of contributing to a retirement plan or you have money to invest, equities can be a strong part of your portfolio. For the past few years, I have been increasing my position in high-dividend-yielding strong stocks. Here is why and how, but first read this carefully: I am only telling you what I am doing, not teaching you to be a professional money manager. So don't read this and go out and buy stocks right away! Use this information as a tool to learn. At this point in time, bonds yield next to nothing and money markets pay nothing; in order to earn anything on investments, you must be extremely diligent.

As I said earlier in the book, I believe you should always have some cash on hand to buy stocks when they are priced right. I have no more than ten to twelve stocks that I track. If I had more time, I might add a few more, but this is about all I can keep track of properly as I am putting hours in at work, writing, and settling into a new house. You must learn the fundamentals before you go out and gamble in the stock market—yes, I said gamble, because if you buy stocks without properly learning the fundamentals, you really are just gambling. Say you are just looking at charts. Charts are kind of like driving; looking through the rearview mirror is a great tool to help you while driving, but unless you are looking at where you are going, you will most likely crash.

I believe you need to know as much as you can to be the best investor you can. Here are the tips I will break down for you. First, know the company you want to buy as intimately as you can; study everything about it. If you can, go and make purchases at the business and see how the service is and the total customer experience. Second, you need to study the stock. You should look at the financials and charts, and constantly read as much information as you can on a daily basis. Third, you should look at things like inventory. The inventory a company has or does not have can be an indicator of how upcoming sales may be headed. Fourth, look at businesses that support your company. For example, if you own a tech stock and one of their suppliers reports earnings and shows that they had an increase in orders for the chips that they make, it could indicate that your company expects to sell more. Look at companies in the same sector; sometimes an entire industry may be doing well or poorly. Take a look at retailers if the winter weather is extremely bad in a large part of the country and people there can't or won't be shopping as much. Earnings are key. If a business that supports your company reports lower-than-expected earnings and then lowers

[Tales of an American Entrepreneur]

their forecast for the rest of the year, this could tell you ahead of time that the stock you own may be headed lower as well.

So, how do you get this information? Well, you have to get dialed in. Check out Google; look for information on the stock you want to purchase. Type in the name of the business and see where Google takes you. Go to the business website. Try Fidelity, Schwab, Vanguard—all of the investment companies provide a lot of information. Check out Motley Fool; I found them to be helpful. I get articles from Seeking Alpha, and they are in my opinion very helpful. Look at Squawk on the Street; keep in mind it is TV and they need to have ratings, so they tend to give you a lot of negative and positive hype nonsense. Cramer's Mad Money is entertaining, and if you listen to what Jim says, he can give you a lead on a stock that has good upside potential. He can also warn you if the stock looks like it may be headed south. Take a stock he recommends buying or selling, and don't just go and pull the trigger. Go and do your homework. Jim has given you an opportunity to look at a stock; it is your responsibility to see if that opportunity makes sense.

The market goes up and down each day. Television programs won't just say, "Yesterday the market had big gains for the third day in a row, so it is headed down today as people are taking some profit." My point is, and has been throughout this book, that you need to teach yourself. When the market is down, TV reporters will tell you things are horrible, but that is what you have been preparing for; this is why you have been doing the homework I have asked you to do. With all the information you have studied, you should know if the stock you have been tracking now presents a good buying or selling opportunity. Furthermore, if the stock is trading at an all-time high, you should know if it is becoming overvalued; does this present a time to take some profit?

I read a book by Peter Lynch, who was a great investor with Fidelity. His approach was to buy the stocks you know, such as Target or McDonalds. How about Clorox? Peter wrote something to the effect of, "If you don't fully understand what the companies do, why would you lay your money down?" You need to constantly study the financials of the company.

I talked earlier in this book about profit and loss. Let's take McDonalds, ticker symbol MCD. McDonalds is a fast-food restaurant everyone in this country knows. McDonalds is the largest fast-food restaurant chain in the world, with over 33,000 stores. We all know the menu: Big Mac, fries, cheeseburger, shakes ... but did you know that the stock has an extremely impressive growth over the past fifteen years? You know the menu; now learn about the company as a business and learn the stock.

Did you know that MCD has consistently paid a dividend and raised their dividends over time? Currently as I am writing this book, MCD pays a 3.14 percent dividend. The company has potential growth in Europe, China, and other parts of the world. The company reports earnings, as all do, and you need to know what to look for that could drive or hurt earnings. A strong dollar could potentially hurt global businesses that expect the bigger part of growth from outside the United States.

How about food costs? Rising food costs can shrink profits. What about the economy in general? A slowing economy could force people to scale down and eat more frequently at fast-food restaurants; on the other hand, if things get too tight or gas prices rise, people may not be as inclined to go even for fast food. So in order to study MCD, you need to not only learn all about McDonalds, but you need to look at how companies are doing that supply McDonalds and what is going on in other parts of the world.

Once you understand this, you also need to know how a stock is valued. At what point is MCD considered expensive or cheap? In other words, when do you buy it and when do you sell it? Knowing one or a few of the things I mentioned is not enough. Remember Gordon Geiko from the movie *Wall Street*? Michael Douglas tells Charlie Sheen that information is power. Well, this is what he is talking about. Okay, so he was talking about even more information—insider information that got him arrested, and we are not talking about that. If you want to be a successful investor, you need to study everything that can impact your stock.

General Mills (GIS) is another stock that pays a dividend. You know Cheerios well. The stock has been a steady grower and pays a dividend. When you look at a stock chart, always look for the bottom price; look at the dips. You may see that a stock may be trading at its high, but if you look back a year or two or longer, you might see that it was trading at that price or higher. Once you understand the charts a bit more, you can look for the dips; this will help you see how the stock traded, which can help you determine your strike price or price to purchase it at.

In the case of GIS, I had an order that I placed as a good-to-cancelled, meaning that I picked a specific price I would pay for the stock and the order would continue until it either hit my price and the trade would be executed or I canceled the order. I had that order for many months, and finally the stock came down to my price and I got it. The stock was taken down by the market in general. The market had several down days, and sometimes it brings down the price of a stock that is doing well and really should not be down. You need to know your stock and read stories and headlines every day because you don't want to have an open order and then find out that the company missed earnings by a lot. This will bring the price down and could be considerably less than your strike price.

So how do you place the trade?

Here are the trade categories for a buy order:

Market order—A market order will buy you the stock at whatever price it is trading at.

Limit order—A limit order will allow you to set a price you are willing to pay for the stock and will execute the trade at that price.

Here are the sell order categories:

Market—A sell market order is generally used when you have a stock that is declining and you need to get out now; it will sell at whatever the price is.

Limit—A limit is used when you want to control the sales price. You set your limit, and if the stock gets to that price, the trade would be executed.

Stop limit—If you have XYZ stock and want to protect your position from decline, you can place an order to sell at a certain price. Whatever price you set, let's say one hundred dollars, if the stock drops to one hundred, the stop is triggered and becomes a limit order so if the stock hits one hundred and goes higher, the order should not be executed. If it hits one hundred and keeps going lower, it will not be executed either.

It needs to go to one hundred again to execute. A stop limit will not protect against a sharp drop. Let's say your stock is at $100.00 and you have a stop limit at $95.00; if it opens sharply lower, say at $90.00, and keeps tanking, your order will not execute.

Stop Market—A stop market becomes a market order when the trigger number is reached and will sell at market price. This could be above if it hits the trigger price and then goes higher, or it can be lower if it keeps dropping.

I had a situation with Apple. They were scheduled to report earnings after the bell, and I wanted to protect my position. I thought if they missed their earnings forecast, the stock would drop. The trouble was, I had no way to know how far and could not predict with any certainty where to put my stop order; ultimately it would need to be lower than I wanted if I was protecting. I decided not to put the sell order because I had conviction that even if they missed, enough things were happening that the stock would go higher as reports from other companies indicated more inventory for Apple for the next quarter.

My position was short-term, and I wanted to hold longer because they would have to have dropped a lot just for me to pay the taxes. Taxes are not the sole reason to hold, but in the case of Apple at that time, they were. Lo and behold, they made their numbers with some room to spare, and the price continued up.

I can't take all the credit. I have to give some to my broker as we had a conversation that afternoon about it and we came to the conclusion that we would hold tight.

I teach my children to never place a market order. A market order will pay whatever the price is when you place your order, and this can change rapidly. The price could rise a lot before your order gets executed. Instead, I use a limit order; this allows me to control the price I want to pay. Kids learn so quickly; their minds are incredible. I want to teach my children how to save and invest so they will be way ahead of where I was when they enter adulthood. I was taught through trial and error by myself. I want to be my children's mentor and give them as much of a start as I can.

I recommend as an exercise that you trade hypothetically before using your money. I also recommend that when you are starting out, you make small trades. Remember, this is not getting rich quick! Many people go into buying stocks with false expectations. We hear of all the Wall Street tycoons who make millions of dollars, and yes, they do exist, but they did not do it on their first trade. Take the Olympics. This is a platform on which the best of the world compete. Do you think this is the first time they ever swam or mounted a pommel horse? It takes many years of practicing many hours *every* day. So start slow and develop your skill set trading maybe ten to twenty shares.

If you understand the fundamentals and are looking to trade actively, start at first trading enough to cover your trades. By this, I mean it will cost you about seven to ten dollars to buy a stock and the same when you sell. So just try to make enough to cover your trade plus the tax you will have to pay. If you have a short-term trade, you will be paying short-term capital gains; this translates into being taxed at your income tax rate. If you hold the stock long enough to qualify for long-term gains, you will be taxed at 15 percent. This is a whole lot better in most cases.

I have found when it comes to investing that patience is one of my greatest allies. Remember earlier in this book I told you about Donald Trump's lesson that you get your best deal when you are willing to walk away from it? Do not get trapped into thinking you have to own that stock now. Stick to your research and buy it when it is at your price. If you are doing your research correctly, you are tracking (learning about) six to twelve companies. So do not get emotional about any.

Here is an example. Let's say you are looking at Apple, MCD, KMR, and XOM. What if one of these, say Apple, starts moving to the upside and posts big gains. Do you raise your purchase price? How about if the oil industry gets some bad press, prices come down, and XOM starts falling? Before you buy and sell stocks, you should do all the fact-finding you can and know these stocks intimately such that if this were to happen, you would know to buy or pass.

No one has a crystal ball, but if you are properly prepared, you stand a much better chance of achieving your desired outcome. If while you are reading this, you are thinking, "I will never have the time to do all this," well, then you are right. If you are reading this and you are thinking, "I can't wait to get started. I am interested in this or that stock. I am going to start right now finding out as much as I can and

I will be able to do this," well, then you are right. It takes a *lot* of time and persistence, but you eat an elephant one bite at a time.

Rule number 1: Never pay too much for a stock. Buy high, sell low just won't make it!

Rule number 2: Never become emotional with your investments. No matter how much you may like a business, if it is time to sell, it is time to sell! On the other hand, if the fundamentals look good and the stock is being brought down by the overall market, don't worry.

Rule number 3: Never chase a stock! If the price of a stock is going up for no concrete reason, don't just randomly raise your purchase price. Usually if the stock is just going higher on momentum, it will retreat to more reasonable levels. If you chased it, you could find yourself wishing you'd stuck to your guns.

Rule number 4: *Never* gamble; to me buying a stock because someone told you about it or because the chart looks good or for any reason other than you thoroughly learned all you could about it is gambling.

CHAPTER 16
Losing Top Employees

It seems it is inevitable that at some point in your business, you will lose top-performing employees. There are many things that change in life that we cannot control. You may have an employee who meets someone that lives in another state, and he or she decides to get married and live in the other state. People relocate for many reasons and more often than you think. Losing a top-performing employee is bad and hard enough when the reason is for life changes, but you also can lose them on unpleasant terms.

Having a key employee leave your business can be one of the most stressful and trying times for any business owner, believe me, I know. As I told you earlier in the book, I once got sick from having employees quit. This is such a stressful topic, it scares me to write about it. So let me help you learn from M.E.—my experience. I did not know it then, but over the years, I have learned a few things.

First and foremost is that God does care for you, and if he is the center of your life and you have a relationship with him, even though the time may seem hard, he is with you, carrying you.

Next, consider this: odds are in your favor that when you lose employees, your profit will rise in the short term. I said odds are in your favor that profits will increase in the short term. That does not mean every time, but more often than not. Let me tell you about the time I opened a flagship location, and shortly after two of my highest producers quit. I had just signed a very high lease and spent hundreds of thousands of dollars on a new location, and two of my top producers left. Lucky for me that I had many years in business and experienced this before, or I believe I would have had a mental and physical breakdown. They left, and that year was the highest-revenue year my business ever had up till then.

So please, if this happens to you, just stop and take a deep breath; everything will be all right. You must continue on as if everything were okay. You need to show leadership to your employees and vendors. Continue to drive your business, even though you want to curl up in a ball and just pass out! Even as I am writing this book. my general manager has left; she felt called to go work at her church. I wished her well—how could I argue against that? Yes, we parted on good terms, but I am still without a manager. As if that were not hard enough, my assistant manager's fiancé took a job in Connecticut, and she moved as well! I did hire another assistant but she did not work out, and now I must do the entrepreneur shuffle and work seventy-five to eighty hours a week!

Let's just throw one in for those who think that it is not fair for anyone to earn over the randomly chosen number that President Obama and his council picked. I have put so much into growing my business, there is not enough memory in this computer to describe it, and I did not do it so I could earn pennies or to place me on the same earnings level with the greeter at Wal-Mart! It absolutely infuriates me to hear that my government wants me to give more (a higher percent) of what I have worked so hard for so they can squander it as they please under the cover of redistribution!

If people worked for the money they have earned, shouldn't they be the ones to decide what to do with it? Shouldn't you get to decide what charity you want to help or what people you want to give money to? I am not suggesting not paying any taxes. I do understand the government needs to provide for defense, as well as certain infrastructure, and government does have an important role that does require money. However, the government claims that the rich need to "pay their fair share."

Well, first let's define *rich*. Some people in government want to arbitrarily pick a number. Today the number appears to be earning two hundred and fifty thousand dollars a year. Let's clearly put that into perspective. President Barak Obama has stated on numerous occasions that the wealthy do not need a tax break and also suggests Warren Buffet does not need a tax break. Well, Warren Buffet has consistently ranked as one of the *world's* richest people. His earnings are more in line with $250,000.00 a minute at the average person's forty-hour week. He also states that Warren Buffet said trickledown economics does not work; however, what he leaves out is that Warren Buffet was talking about wealthy people who are not affected by tax consequences relative to whether or not they will make a purchase. To reach that kind of critical mass, one needs to have even on the low end hundreds of millions of dollars available.

Remember, Warren Buffet has friends like Bill Gates, and together they have ranked among the world's top ten wealthiest people for many years. They each have tens of billions of dollars. This is a class that 99 percent of the people on the planet earth cannot even begin to understand. So please, do not even try to put the hardworking and sacrificing person who is earning a decent living in the same boat.

It is important when trying to look at a tax structure that is conducive to productivity that we do not keep the ceiling low. What do you think a high-earning annual salary is? Some may say fifty thousand; still others would say one hundred thousand. How about two or three hundred thousand? Take a moment to think about the lifestyle you would live at, say, two hundred thousand dollars annual income. A nice house for your family, new car, maybe one used car, furniture, children, clothes, food, utilities, sports, entertainment … oh and most likely you would still have a mortgage, school loans, car loan, and yes, still be trying to save for emergencies and retirement.

I believe the more people who work to earn their way to a higher income without being penalized in the way of higher taxes and taking away standard deductions, like a home mortgage, saving for retirement, and saving for school, the more money will flow to the economy and we will see a higher standard of life for everyone.

Still don't believe me? Let's think about how we live in America and look at how people live in India or countries in Africa. Even our poor have much higher income than the poor in those countries. We as a country have a much higher standard of living. Instead of the government taking money from private citizens and keeping it in the government, how much better off would people be if the citizens kept more of their earned money?

People, just give this a thought: you may work hard your whole life and pay taxes on all that you have earned, with the intent of passing your money on to your children. So far, that sounds like it is right, doesn't it? Well, when you die, the government will tax whatever you have accumulated and sometimes even confiscate half of it! How does this help your children in any way?

Let me say this again for the person who wants to control and oppress people by saying, "Well, if you earn x amount, you can afford to pay more taxes." This is how government can keep people from moving up the economic ladder. I suggest they move the bar way higher so that if they want to determine an income level on which to charge higher taxes, it is truly on a high income.

How about not having the government charging more income tax, but instead having government spend less? How about being responsible for yourself and not wanting to live off other people? Because that is what you do when you think the government will pay for things you need or want. Government does not produce income. They simply take it from someone else. Some of you say, "Well, that is okay." But how about they just take more from you? Our country should require our elected officials to have worked in business as an owner or high-ranking executive, or at the very least, require that they can reconcile and balance their own checkbooks! The point is that there are so many obstacles you must overcome to be successful in business that you must look at it as just another level in the game.

I don't want to get political, but I urge anyone who is planning to vote to give due diligence to this precious right. Don't just vote for the person on your team. Take the time to research candidates. If they are already politicians, look at their voting records. This is not hard to do. You can go to their website and sign on to the newsletter. Or how about writing them a letter about a topic of your concern? Then you can see how they respond. If they are not career politicians, you can still find out a lot about candidates; just Google their name.

Another idea is to require voters to pass a simple quiz before they vote. It could be as simple as naming the current president and vice president, and at least one senator or one congressman from the state the voter resides in. Another question that should be asked is what the three branches of government are. I know you may think that is so naïve, but if a voter can't answer that, do you think he or she would know the record of a candidate? I think that encouraging people to educate themselves by having them answer a few fundamental questions without penalty would, if nothing else, get them to be more involved in a constructive way. So even if they don't know the correct answer, they can still vote. These questions could be sent with their voter card.

Now then, back to staff issues. My best advice regarding employees is to have replacements on hand, someone who can fill the position. No, I am not suggesting you should be wage-heavy, but rather train and cross-train your employees so in the event you need to, you can promote from within. I know that is extremely hard, and I too get caught short sometimes if an employee terminates his or her position or is terminated, but this is the easiest remedy. Next, don't panic. Roll up your sleeves and get to work! You did not become an entrepreneur thinking it would be a cakewalk, did you? Prioritize your situation and continue doing what is needed. You will find the right people.

I might have been writing that last paragraph for myself, as I have reviewed it often these past months. It is now seven months after my GM resigned, and I now have an assistant manager who for the past month and a half has been doing well; I hope to promote him to the manager level in a few weeks! I have not written for the past seven months as I have been covered up with managing and running my business and any downtime I get is for my family and to daily give glory, honor, and thanks to God.

So, let me give you an idea of what I have been doing since I have not written for at least seven months. (What do you do with your time?) I have been working at the salon six days a week open to close. On Sundays and at night, I had been doing my office work for the first few months. About two months after my general manager left, my wife and I were able to get more of a routine down, as she became better at opening and scheduling appointments; since she was a morning person, she opened, and I would come in around noon till close, usually 8:30 p.m.

In the beginning of this book, I stated that I owned a company and that I did not have to be at the store all the time. This is the business model I strive for and have been quite successful at it for many years. If you are looking to open multiple locations, this all becomes even harder.

First, remember you must absolutely have management in line to take up the slack in the event of employee turnover.

Second, you must continue to train your employees in the best possible manner. Never ever stop training. Let's say a manager quits, and you have one or even a few locations. If your next in line can't perform those duties, you may see your business standards drop. It is extremely hard to uphold high standards when your employees are not capable of delivering that level of service. You will occasionally see this in businesses if you look. Take a small restaurant when the manager leaves; you sometimes see that they do not have the same level of service, it is not as clean, or they consistently mess up your order. Your customers may forgive you once, but by the second time, they will have already found another place that can give them what they want.

Third, you must have a business culture that you also continue to develop. How do you treat customers? What are your expectations? What are your policies? Every employee must be taught how he or she should perform. The small business owner will not likely have the time to train new people and step into the manager's role as well as do what they do in times of crisis. You must have systems in place so you can continue to grow your business even in times of a shorthanded crisis.

CHAPTER 17
Let's Take a Look at Customer Service

This is a topic that everyone talks about, but in everyday experiences, it seems no one knows anything about it. I want to tell you a story about a restaurant that I have gone to many times. This place has great food. They serve Greek-styled food; while not traditional, it does have the influence. I have never eaten there and said it did not taste good. Okay, so why am I telling you about this? So what? Lots of restaurants have consistently good food.

I'm telling you about this restaurant because it has been one too many times that the service has been absolutely horrible; I just cannot go back anymore. When I call in an order to go, they consistently give me the wrong order or no utensils, or they don't have it when I walk in and pay for it. Instead, they hand it to people who walk in after me and place the same order. They usually have several people behind the counter, none of whom acknowledge any customers and only one working the register, even if ten people are on line; the others do nothing.

I see poor customer service in many businesses, but people accept it. Just think about how many times you go to a department store or home improvement store. You have the hardest time finding anyone who works there, and when you do, the employee is not able to answer any questions because he or she has absolutely no product knowledge. Or if you ask where an item is, the employee points and says, "over on aisle 35." Well, most of the time, aisle 35 is half a block long and has over a thousand items on it!

I was in a wine store looking for a particular wine, and if they had had it, I would have purchased a case. I was in an aisle that had

California Cabernet, and I was just looking for a few other specific wines when I was approached by a salesperson. He asked, "Can I help you?" And I replied, "Yes, I am looking specifically for an Italian wine." I told him which one and asked if he had it. He then said, "Well, you're not in the right aisle. The Barolos are in the Italian section," and he started walking as if I would follow. I just turned and continued my search for Duckhorn Cabernet.

He then told me I needed to follow him, and I politely replied, "No, I will not. You asked if you could help me. I would like you to see if you have this particular wine for me. That would be helpful. Could you please check for me?" He then said he would. Fifteen minutes later, I walked over to the section that would have the Barolo I was searching for only to see this guy looking at the shelves. I found a Sangiovese that I wanted, and he then walked up to me and said he had a wine that was good. I did appreciate the try, but through our brief conversation, I knew he had no idea about wine nor had he drunk the one he was suggesting; he was just reading the comment card to me. I politely told him that I could read and that I appreciated his effort but I would like to look on my own.

If this person had been trained properly, he could have sold me a lot of wine, and not just on that visit. If I had had a good experience, I would go back and tell other people to go there, and I am just one customer Look at how you can multiply your customer base simply by teaching your employees properly. Sure, I could probably write a book on bad customer service, and in a sense, it is the topic. Take note of the service you receive when you go to a business, be it a restaurant or retail store or wherever you go. Make notes of bad service and make sure you do not do the same thing in your business. On the flip side, make notes of good service and duplicate it in your business. Here are some great ways to learn customer service:

1. Look around every time you purchase anything. What did you like or dislike about the experience? How would you have made it better, and how could you implement that in your business? Ask friends about their shopping and dining experiences. What was bad? What was good?

2. Go to places that have world-class customer service—Disney, Westin Hotel Resorts, MGM Grand in Las Vegas, Delfrisco's Double Eagle Steak House, just to name a few. Each of these places does unique things with customer service. Take Disney, for example. Stay at one of the resorts in Disney World, and then go back several years later. Here is what I experienced when I called to book another stay about two or three years later. The person I was speaking with said, "Mr. Randazzo, how are your daughters?" and he called them by name. "Are they excited to come back to Disney? I see you stayed at the Floridian. Will you be booking that resort again?" Talk about knowing your customer and making him or her feel important! How about Emeril's? My wife had dinner there and noticed that they did not refill her water glass; they simply replaced it, even when she did not drink much from it but the ice had melted. Learn from other businesses that are masters at world-class customer service. Treat yourself and take note of everything they do. But remember, you must implement what you learn in your business.
3. A great training tool for staff can be to send them to a restaurant that you know has great service as a reward for high sales. Think of a bonus structure that will reward your top performers with an overnight stay at a resort. If you want your employees to deliver great service, they need to have experienced it, or at the least you will need to train them. Tell them what to say and show them what to do. Use role-playing. I believe this is a great way to get them to feel comfortable doing what is expected of them. Do not overlook anything when it comes to how you want your customers treated. Take a look at Starbucks. They train their employees to use the words tall, venti, and grande. This is such a key to the Starbucks experience. If they used small, medium, and large, it would not set them apart and would not help them charge more for coffee. Even such small things as this have a profound impact on customers.
4. Get going with your business. Don't wait until you have the ultimate customer service system. Start with a plan and improve it as often as necessary. Poll your customers. Ask them to give

you ideas on what could improve your service. At Harmony Salon, we send e-mail feedback forms to all our clients and ask them at the end for suggestions on what we could do to improve. Do not get emotional. If they tell you something that does not make you warm and fuzzy, remember: you asked them. Instead, try to understand their suggestion and see if it makes sense or if it sparks an idea that you can do that will work for your business. We use our positive feedback forms to post in the break room or e-mail to our employees or just tell them. I like to take the positive and roll it through our store to keep people thinking positive. I believe that we need to put out what we want. It is so easy for employees and customers to complain, and I don't want to stay focused on what I do not want. If I do get a negative form, I usually will meet with that employee and go over it with him or her. I keep a folder for each employee so I can benchmark and see how many and what types of feedback each employee is getting. This way I can see patterns and know if there needs to be technical or customer experience training needed for any employees.

5. Read often. There are so many great books that can open your eyes to great customer service. I will give you a few recommendations, starting with the book you are reading now. The next book that I think of when I think of marketing and customer service is *What's the Secret?* written by John R. Dijulius. John's book has a wealth of knowledge in it. He will tell you so many things you can do to step up your customer service and market your business. If you get a chance to hear him speak, don't miss it, as he is a great speaker and a marketing guru. He will get you pumped with ideas. *Married to the Brand* by William J. McEwen, *Emotional Branding* by Marc Gobe, and *Trading Up* by Michael J. Silverstein are also good sources to help you understand how businesses can be more than just the service or product they provide.

So, exactly what is customer service? In the pure and simple meaning, it is how a business services its customers. Many people think that the words *customer service* mean that the customer can have or do anything he or she wants. However, we know that is not the case. There are many different types of customer service, and you must decide what your customer service will be.

Will you be a barbershop that has customers walk in, sit down, read a magazine till it is their turn, and then talk junk with the barber, get the same haircut they have always had, then pay and leave—or will you be a salon that takes appointments as well as walk-ins? The salon can provide refreshments while customers wait; it can give a free massage, hand treatment, hot towel facial, or makeup touch-up as a value-added service.

There is no right or wrong in how you position your business; however, do not expect it to be what it is not. You won't be able to sustain a profitable business that charges top price but delivers bottom service. I will tell you this: the higher up you go in the customer service level, the more is expected from you by your customers, so take the emotion out of it and learn to deal with all sorts of customer complaints. What I mean is learn from the complaints; look between the lines.

We are human, and when someone complains or is negative, our natural instinct is to tell him or her where to go. Instead, bite your tongue and hear what he or she is saying. Then figure out how to prevent that complaint from happening again by developing your systems. I do not suggest that you compromise your integrity; there are occasions when it is best to politely invite a customer to go somewhere else, but it is only the extremely bad client that you want to not return. Yes, I said bad client, and there are times when the customer is not right.

I will tell you how we deal with the bad client in the salon business and how we minimize this behavior. If clients set an appointment and do not show up for it, we call them a no-show. Think about it: your service provider is now sitting idle because you blocked out two hours for her to do Betty's color and cut and Betty just never came. A few of these, and it can ruin your week and cut your growth. If you get too many of these, it can even put you out of business.

So to cut our no-shows to an absolute minimum, here is what we have done. First, we defined a no-show as canceling with less than a twenty-four-hour notice or not canceling at all. Second, we send out e-mail confirmations a few days before the scheduled appointment. If we do not get a reply, we call the next day; and if we leave a message and do not get a response, we call again the next day. We mark clients that no-show so we can keep track of this. If a client no-shows more than three times in eight appointments or if he or she is new and no-shows the first three times, we ask for a credit card to guarantee the reservation time and let the client know we will bill him or her if there is not a twenty-four-hour cancelation or reschedule notice. Some get offended, and we do not book them; some understand and have no problem.

In the end, if someone is not going to respect your time, you need to find a paying customer who will. We also ask clients when scheduling appointments to kindly give a twenty-four-hour notice if he or she needs to change or cancel. This is an example of how customer service helps you increase revenue. Needless to say, we cut our no-shows dramatically. We see just about two thousand clients a month. If we are to grow to three thousand a month, we will continue to do what we do well, and more than likely implement new systems, some of which we will probably develop from customer challenges or complaints.

CHAPTER 18
Reading My Own Book

It has been a long time since I worked on this book as I have been spending time with my wife and kids, going to church, and working. I now find myself reading my own book. Recently I had two service providers quit, and to add to it, one assistant also quit, all within a few days. So now I have to wonder, how many more are leaving? Sure, I live by the principles I have outlined for you and I am prepared for the ups and downs of business; reading my own story has told me to take a breath and believe it will work out. Still, it is very stressful to have people you see every day just drop a bomb on you without ever talking to you about any concerns they have or even having the decency to leave on good terms.

My faith in God gives me strength, knowing that what really matters is living for him and learning more of him each day. Praying and having a growing relationship with my Lord and Savior is what truly matters. I had trouble sleeping and watched *The Passion of the Christ*; it was horrifying to see and understand the mob mentality that killed a man who preached love and kindness. Jesus taught man to live by God's Word, and for that, he was hung alongside criminals. Think about it: the amazing thing is that he never showed anger to those that were beating him and torturing him, but instead, beaten, bloody, with nails driven through his hands and feet, he prayed for those that were killing him. He prayed for God to forgive them. Wow, it is mind-blowing how he was able to stay on course and complete a way for us all to be with God. He completed the way; all we have to do is choose.

As I see things today in person and in the news, not much has changed since then. We live in a world that wants to live away from God and wants to persecute those who live for him. People love to destroy good businesses. People will write and say the nastiest things about a business with no regard for what they really were not happy with. I see it in my business and in others.

A few days ago, the CEO of Chick-fil-A stated his personal opinion of marriage and said that he thought our country was inviting God's wrath when man shakes his fist at him and says, "We know better than you how to define marriage." His statement comes from the Bible that marriage is a covenant with God. Now why is he not entitled to his opinion? People went nuts, spewing hatred and calling to boycott his business. It made national news. Chick-fil-A is the only fast-food business I know of that is closed on Sunday. This business is following the Sabbath as God instructed.

I don't know why some people want to change how we define marriage; from what I know, it is about benefits. People want to be able to extend benefits that are currently designated for married couples, like social security and health care. I see no problem with this, but I think this should be taken up with government, not the church. I know that this is a hot topic, but I think attacking God or religion is attacking the wrong place. I think that if you want to provide health insurance for anyone, you should be able to add him or her to your policy. I also think that if you want to have your social security go to anyone you choose if you should die, it should be so.

I guess my point is that government should be the one petitioned for this. These benefits, if you want to call them that, were traditionally provided to married couples. I think you should be able to provide for anyone you see fit. So does it have to be that they attack the definition of marriage? I don't believe so. Now on the other hand, if people want to break a covenant with God and want those who have strong religious convictions to accept it just because they want to, well, I think that is wrong. It is, in fact, what they wanted to stop from happening—bullying, persecuting, and forcing your belief on someone else.

Is that really what we should be doing? Christ came for us all; he did not demand, though he well could have. His love and forgiveness are there for anyone who will ask, regardless of who he or she is and what he or she has done. We do not force our belief on anyone, for God's mercy is his alone. Marriage between a man and a woman is how it has been since the beginning of humanity. So we do not force this covenant, but honor it as we have always. If we turned this around and had marriage between only two men or two women, then there would be no one to argue the point of marriage between a man and a woman. Nor would there be any marriage at all, as human beings would cease to exist.

So I am saying marriage is a covenant with God, and this can't be changed. People should be free to place anyone they choose on their health insurance or social security (if social security is even worth anything in the near future). These are things for government; religious covenants are for the church. I hear people saying it is a culture thing. I don't know what that means, so I still have no idea why people want to invade religious covenants and destroy them. What about changing government so it does not oppress people and keep them from reaching their potential?

I hear people say that Jesus said, "Above the commandments are these two: love God and love your neighbor." In perspective, Jesus told a woman accused of adultery to go and sin no more. He did not say it was all right and go and continue to do whatever it was she wanted to do. So, loving your neighbor does not mean to condone any and everything he or she does.

To understand Christ, you need to get dialed in, just like understanding anything. How can people profess to be of a certain faith when they have not read and studied their Bible? The Bible is a very large book, and if you only look at one or two sentences from the book, you will not know all that is written. For that matter, if you read only one or two books of the Bible, you will not know. There is so much to absorb, and many things may take time to understand. For me, I think if you ask the question, "Why are we here; is there a creator?" it then sets you on a path that may take your entire lifetime to answer, but if you truly ask and search, you will discover so much that you did not know.

I don't want you to think that I think I know it all. I certainly do not have all the answers. I am just sharing what I have learned—and just for the record, I have read and continue to read the Bible in its entirety, and I still learn almost every time I read it.

I want to get back to my point of what you will deal with in your business. Yes, strangely enough, not only the fundamental business functions, like inventory, customers, financials, and employees, but also terrorist attacks, world markets, and the guiding principles that not only you have but other principles that others have as well. For example, what will you do to ensure your business can handle terrorists knocking down the World Trade Center and as a result shutting down trading at the New York Stock Exchange for a week? How will this impact your business, or will it have any impact on your business? The principles that you run your business by, others may not agree with, so do you change or hold fast to your beliefs? You will have to decide. Let me show you some of what I am talking about.

I have a friend who is in banking, and she occasionally vents to me, telling me the abusive profanities people scream at her. Some of her customers are just plain mean, ugly nasty to her, and the things they are mad about have nothing to do with her. She does not make the rules or policy. She is a good person with honor and should not be treated like that. I often wonder why people behave as they do, and I evaluate myself when I behave in a manner that is not how I want to conduct myself. In the least, this helps me to control my emotions and broaden my ability to overcome challenges. Yes, I still sometimes lose my cool and react instead of interact.

Another friend I know owns a pizza restaurant, and he has told me how people will scream at him, saying every time they come in, they have problems, they don't like the food, it's too this or that. He has told the same story to my banker friend. My thought is, why do they keep coming back? Why not go make someone else miserable? This man works seven days a week and has a great product; his pizza is one of the best around, and his eggplant is fantastic. His restaurant is always very busy. He told me a story that his food costs went up, shipping went up, and rent and other costs went up as well, so he had to raise his price on some items and only by a nickel. Well, some people actually complained and gave him a hard time. A nickel! It is unbelievable how many people are penny-wise and dollar-foolish.

I hear the news and see that some people think nothing of the government taking your money, maybe because they think they will get something for free. I wonder if these people hold themselves to the same standards as they dish out spewing their hate and misery. Think about this: imagine hearing from your friend or coworker such complaints as, "I hate my boss; he is getting on me for being late. My job is horrible; they are constantly getting on me about sanitation guidelines. I have to hear junk all the time from work about the dress code. My job stinks. I have to get this work done by Friday." Now here is the real kicker for me: most reasonably sane people and truly Christ-centered people will say, "Well, why do you get to work late?" An honorable person would tell the complainer that he or she should be written up or fired. Who wants someone spreading disease or spoilage by not following proper sanitation?

Still, it seems that more people will just jump on the mob mentality and embrace the destructive, hateful "oh you should quit" or "that place sucks." They never think at all about what they themselves stand for and who they are cutting down. It is our choice! We can live a purpose-filled life aimed at eternity or a life of debauchery, not thinking about what we are doing with each day and how we will be judged. If you are in business, whether in management or if you own a business, you will come up against horrible stress; and it is my belief that if you don't have sound principles and a strong faith in God, the stress will be overwhelming. In my journey, I spoke to you about some successful companies and gave you things you can learn from them.

Now I want to tell you about another friend, who owned a mattress company in Arizona. He had this business for many years, manufacturing mattresses and selling them mostly wholesale. As you can imagine, when the housing market crashed and took the economy with it, the mattress business crashed as well, as did many other businesses. Business can be brutal, and even the best-prepared businesses sometimes cannot withstand the pressure of no profit. For a small-business person, this can be gut-wrenching, causing depression and many health issues, even heart attack.

So understand this in advance: no matter how well or poorly your business is doing, there is a higher purpose and you should focus on that. God, not the world, should be your litmus test when you make decisions. No matter how good you are doing, someone is doing better, and no matter how bad you have it, someone has it worse.

CHAPTER 19
Over the Years Time Teaches If You Are Smart Enough to Learn

I HAVE OWNED HARMONY Salon for nineteen years and feel compelled to include this chapter, as it is the reason I wanted to write about my journey. I was taught as a child to look at what successful people did and do what they do. I was also taught to do what is right always. My teacher and mentor was then and shall always be the Lord God through his grace Jesus Christ. When I was young, I read Philippians, and when I got to chapter 4 verses 6–9, it had a profound impact on my life. I can remember thinking while reading of honorable things and purposes as I read the words that were recorded in my heart:

> Be anxious for nothing, but in everything by prayer and supplication, with thanksgiving, let your requests be made known to God, and the peace of God which surpasses all understanding will guard your hearts and minds through Christ Jesus. Finally brethren, whatever things are true, whatever things are noble, whatever things are pure, whatever things are lovely, and admirable, whatever things are of good report, if there is any virtue and if there is anything praiseworthy meditate on these things. The things which you have learned and received and heard and saw in me, these do, and the God of peace will be with you.

Can you imagine how this world would be if we followed this

simple teaching? I wonder if there would be any news channels on TV. If so, they would be 100 percent different. Can you imagine people's conversations? No more gossip, no more backstabbing, no more just plain mean and ugly tear-people-down talk! How would people conduct themselves if they thought about those few words daily?

This brings me to where I am now in my business: one more stylist quit. We spoke, and she told me she wanted to pursue a dream of working on movie sets and that she has the opportunity to do this. She said she would be in effect giving me about a month's notice. I told her if she were telling the truth and was honorable that during that time, she could suggest some of her coworkers for the clients she was working on and that if things did not work out, she would always be welcome. Well, that was not the case. She was getting clients' phone numbers and giving clients her phone number and telling them about another salon she was going to work at where she would be renting a chair. Needless to say, I let her go as soon as I found out.

I have to tell you about the stress I am going through so you can understand that other business owners do experience this and to different degrees. My hope is that you will use this book as a guide to try to avoid these situations if you can and to help you through them if you can't. So here I am. I have had my business for almost twenty years. I have worked at times so many hours per week that I did nothing else. My business has lasted through many challenging and hard times.

We have lost key employees, and we watched in horror as the World Trade Center was struck and fell, the Pentagon, was hit, and we were attacked by terrorists. There was a time when I had to close because we were all sick with the flu. We survived through the major stock market crashes and the worst economic depression our country has ever had.

I had about a third of my staff quit without notice, and this is what happened. I found myself beginning to panic; my heart began to race, my stomach was in knots, and I felt tension throughout my entire body. My stomach was the worst, and lying in bed, my body was twitching; my legs, my arms, everything was just locked up. Now I think everyone deals with stress as a natural part of life, but this kind of intense stress is worse; my mind brought fear front and center.

Do you remember near the beginning of this book when I described the stress that fear was causing me and how I now refer to it as success fear? I tried to overcome it, but it just got worse. So the science behind it is something like this: at these intense stress encounters, your brain releases hormones, peptides, neurotransmitters, and other chemicals that can paralyze you in that moment. Neurotransmitters are messengers that pass information from nerve cells to other parts of your body to allow a specific function.

When the first employee quit and then a few days later the next, these transmitters caused my brain to think of all the other times this had happened as well as other similar situations. This fed on itself, causing me to fear who else would quit. Then another person did quit, and the fear just kept getting worse. Then there is another part of the nervous system, the sympathetic nervous system. This is part of the automatic nervous system in the middle of your brain and is responsible for automatic responses you can't control.

My body was subconsciously thinking it was under threat, but I didn't think of it that way. My thoughts became clouded, and I couldn't rationalize. My body kept releasing more emotions, and my brain became overwhelmed. This can go on for days, and if you don't shake it, it can break down your immune system, leaving you vulnerable to sickness and heart attack.

Here are things that helped me get my sanity back. I walked briskly in the morning; it gets my heart rate up a little and gets me going. I do push-ups about five or six days per week; this is great for making me feel strong and giving me the fight attitude. I try to eat proper food, fresh not processed and not fast food.

One night I was thinking *I cannot take it anymore*, and my kids asked me to play a Wii game with them. My first thought was that I did not want to play; I wanted to go lock myself in a room and just break down. I knew I had to do something to change my thinking, so we played; and in about twenty minutes or so, I found myself laughing and trying not to get beat too badly by my girls. How wonderful it was to laugh! We played a few games and had a great time, and my mind was starting to get back to a rational state. My stress was subsiding, and I actually was feeling better.

In times of stress, you must change your thoughts. If you allow your thoughts to continue to be negative, you only attract more negative things in your life. My children are my joy, and they always make me feel great, even when inside I am barely able to control my stress. This is the worldly way to approach stress; however, there is also the spiritual way.

In the days that followed, I turned to prayer, as Paul suggested in Philippians to pray all the time.

I had three stylists and one assistant that I had high hopes for quit. The assistant quit just as I was about to promote her to the floor. She was now ready to serve clients, and she quit. When I hired her, she told me she did not want to rent a chair and wanted what my company could provide in career terms. Clearly now she wanted to be trained properly by us only to go work at a place that provided no training, health care, vacation, or any benefits other than she would make her own schedule.

Yes, I was stressed thinking how this would impact my business and what about profit (income). Why did they leave? I thought I was a fair and honest employer. So while I prayed, I asked for the comforter, and instantly my stress was lifted. I knew all would work out and that my Father in heaven was taking care of me. This all happened in the beginning of July, and as I stated earlier in this book, to date (July 21) we are up 10 percent over last year. This past week we had a gain of over 30 percent! Glory and honor and praise God. Payroll costs have gone down, as I told you earlier in this book, and I hired a manager in training. I have a stylist scheduled to start in two weeks, and I have several final interviews for more stylists this week!

I do pray often on my knees first thing when I awake, and just about every day I speak to God.

CHAPTER 20

Being a Blessing to Those in Need

I don't think a single day goes by without someone asking for some kind of donation. Having over thirty thousand people in my data base, you can imagine how many requests I get.

What I try to do before I give is research the charity. What are they accomplishing? How much of what I give goes to the charity? I think the last thing most of us want to see is that we give, but very little of the money we give actually goes to the ones intended!

I recall one charity that called me and said, "Won't you help children with cancer?" My first reaction was probably the same as anyone else: "Yes, I absolutely will help." When I asked for the charity's name and website and if they could provide a financial report, the person hung up on me. I went online and did some digging and found that this was a fund-raising company. After looking further, I found that 70 percent of the money raised went to them and only 30 percent went to the charity.

There are many great organizations helping people, and most are not hard to find. One that I believe truly helps is World Concern. This charity helps bring medicine to children who have parasites from infected water. They also help bring clean water and sanitation to those countries that cannot do it themselves. Another is Pure Religion 5k, which is fighting human trafficking. I think human trafficking is absolutely horrible! Trafficking is slavery, and many of those enslaved are young children who are forced into sex and treated worse than the animals that we see being mistreated on TV.

Whether you feel called to help children, stop cancer, stop domestic abuse, or help people learn about Jesus, whatever you are being called for, do it. Give your time and money, pray, or help in whatever way you can.

CHAPTER 21
What Next?

I HAVE WRITTEN ABOUT some of our best practices and given you some marketing ideas. I talked about real estate, investing, spending, and following dreams. I told and showed you some of the hardest things I have had to deal with as a small-business owner, with the sincere hope that you can learn from me. I encourage you to read the other books I mentioned and reread this one.

If you are opening a business, prepare to work long and hard. It is important to enjoy what you do, for it will be extremely hard to put that effort in if you don't. Take a Spartan approach to your money and know where every nickel goes.

It is now several years that I have been writing this book. Currently we have a manager who is doing great. She has only a few days to go for the quarter and will make her numbers and in turn receive a nice bonus. We have a manager in training, and she is also doing great. We have another person in a front-desk position who will be promoted to the manager-in-training position in a few months, and we also have a new front-desk person we hired about a month ago. So our front is fully staffed. Lisa and I have scaled back the hours that we have been putting in at the salon. Thanksgiving and Christmas are just a few weeks away, and we have so much to be thankful for.

I truly hope you enjoyed reading my journey and learned from reading it. My greatest hope for readers is that they see the amazing plan that God has for each and every one of us, regardless of what you have done, how much money you have, or where you have been. Jesus, yes, read this again, Jesus came for all. Jesus offers forgiveness and acceptance for everyone. You can't buy it or earn it, and we don't even deserve it. All you have to do is pray and tell God you recognize that Jesus was his son and that you want a relationship with God through Christ, and you will be spiritually reborn!

When you give your heart to Christ, you will from then on walk a different path for the rest of your life. You will be on a path that will lead you to God. There are people who do not even recognize God; they are not walking on the same path. All they need to do to see where this path leads is ask Jesus to be their Lord and recognize him as God's son. How easy is that? What a small thing to do.

Imagine how long eternity is. I will give you an example. Imagine all the oceans being emptied and filled with sand as high as Mount Everest. Then imagine once a year a bird flies by and takes one grain of sand. How long would it take for the bird to empty all the sand from all the oceans? That still is not even close to eternity.

You do have a partner in business: God is always there for you and wants you to have your heart's desire.

www.ingramcontent.com/pod-product-compliance
Lightning Source LLC
Chambersburg PA
CBHW030845180526
45163CB00004B/1458

time lag, 86, 93, 107
Total Quality Management, 32
turbulence., 27, 56

U

V

value, iv, 6, 10, 16, 32, 56, 58, 59, 60, 67, 68, 69, 72, 73, 74, 82, 85, 86, 88, 90, 91, 99, 109, 115, 118, 126, 140, 150, 154, 171, 176, 179, 183, 185
value creation, iv, 56, 58, 59, 60, 67, 68, 69, 72, 73, 74, 82, 85, 86, 88, 90, 91, 171, 176, 179, 185
virtual, 16, 71, 80, 85, 86, 90
vision, 6, 9, 10, 11, 12, 13, 14, 17, 33, 174

Ø

O

OECD, 177, 184
organization, 9, 11, 12, 13, 14, 15, 16, 17, 22, 27, 32, 35, 48, 74, 97, 170, 173, 176, 179, 181, 182, 183, 185, 186, 191, 192, 202

P

paradox, 88, 100, 109
pattern., 84
preconditions, 58
premises, 26, 104, 109, 138, 139, 172, 186
projects, 64, 68, 69, 77, 125, 193
punctuation, 137, 147, 187, 199

R

reintegration, 84, 85, 86, 87, 90
relationship-knowledge, 16, 17, 18
requisite variety, 35, 114

S

self-reinforcing, 114
signals, 58, 61, 93, 94, 109, 114, 116, 142
social systems, 39, 45, 47, 61, 68, 78, 102, 103, 106, 107, 108, 110, 112, 118, 121, 127, 130, 131, 135, 143, 151, 162, 170, 188, 191, 193, 196, 197
stability, 18, 63, 101, 106, 120, 123, 128, 138, 151, 178
strategy, 13, 15, 17, 45, 46, 47, 48, 49, 58, 109, 161, 168, 169, 172, 173, 200
symbolic capital, 117
synthesis, 21, 131
Systemic, iv, 23, 101, 118, 192, 194, 196, 198, 200, 201, 207

T

Tacit knowing, 20, 145
Tacit knowledge, 18, 19, 20, 25, 26, 28, 29, 31, 37, 44, 64, 65, 104, 114, 115, 126, 135, 138, 142, 143, 144, 145, 146, 147, 148, 149, 150, 185
technological, 8, 28, 38, 53, 61, 64, 67, 69, 150, 168, 176
technology, 6, 12, 32, 38, 42, 44, 48, 52, 56, 61, 63, 64, 68, 70, 74, 77, 95, 99, 145, 148, 150, 172, 190
theory, iv, v, 6, 10, 11, 38, 39, 42, 45, 49, 56, 86, 97, 105, 106, 108, 111, 112, 128, 130, 131, 140, 151, 156, 159, 160, 167, 186, 189, 195

ABOUT THE AUTHOR

Jon-Arild Johannessen holds a Master of Science from Oslo University in History. He holds a Ph.D. from Stockholm University in Systemic thinking. He is currently professor (full) in Leadership, at Kristiania University College, Oslo and Nord University, Norway. He has been professor (full) in Innovation, at Syd-Danske University, Denmark. He has been professor (full) in Management at The Arctic University, Norway. At Bodø Graduate School of Business, Norway he had a professorship (full) in Information management. At Norwegian School of Management he has been professor in Knowledge Management.

www.ingramcontent.com/pod-product-compliance
Lightning Source LLC
Chambersburg PA
CBHW071812200526
45169CB00017B/168